The Joy of Rhubarb Cookbook

The Versatile Summer Delight

by Theresa Millang

Adventure Publications, Inc.
Cambridge, Minnesota

A special thank you to all who contributed to this cookbook.

Book and Cover Design by Jonathan Norberg

10 9 8 7
Copyright 2004 by Theresa Nell Millang
Published by Adventure Publications, Inc.
820 Cleveland Street South
Cambridge, Minnesota 55008
1-800-678-7006
www.adventurepublications.net
Printed in China
ISBN-13: 978-1-59193-051-8
ISBN-10: 1-59193-051-0

Table of Contents

3

Desserts

Introduction

You know that summer is on the way when the rhubarb stalks are being gathered. You can find this deep red stalk with its broad, bright green leaves growing in back yards, gardens and around old farm buildings. It's doesn't get much attention...until someone remembers their favorite springtime treat...a sauce perhaps.

Yes, this sweetly old-fashioned stalk, with a pucker-sour side, is one of the first joys of summer. The beautiful red stalks can be found in most supermarkets, fresh or frozen, ready to show off their versatility.

Rhubarb can be used alone in recipes or will blend brightly with most fruits. This spirited vegetable (it's not a fruit) is ideal for more than just pies—there are many ways to include this reliable stalk in tasty recipes. Whirl raspberries with rhubarb to create a dessert soup, or pair zesty rhubarb chutney with grilled meat, and, yes, there is still that wonderful strawberry-rhubarb pie!

I have included all of my favorite recipes, and also recipes I have collected from across the country. So, a salute to rhubarb and to all contributors of this collection.

Rhubarb Facts

Ben Franklin is credited for bringing rhubarb seeds to this country in 1772; however, rhubarb was not widely popular until the early 1880s, at which time it was used mostly for making pies and wine. By the mid-1900s it gained popularity that continues to this day.

Rhubarb is a Vegetable
Field-grown rhubarb has cherry-red stalks or petioles and bright green leaves. Hothouse rhubarb has pink to pale red stalks and yellow-green leaves. Field-grown rhubarb has the most pronounced flavor of the two main varieties. Hothouse rhubarb has a milder flavor, and is less stringy. Rhubarb is a perennial; it need not be replanted yearly. It needs a cold season to flourish. Red stalk varieties include Canada Red, Ruby, Valentine, Crimson Wine and Cherry Red. Green stalk varieties include Victoria, German Wine and Sutton's Seedless.

Nutritionally, it is rich in vitamin C, dietary fiber and calcium. However, the amount of calcium that can be absorbed by the body is reduced due to the presence of oxalic acid. Also, rhubarb is naturally low in sugar. One cup of raw rhubarb contains just over a gram of sugar.

Don't Eat The Leaves
Rhubarb stalks look like red stalks of celery. The stalk is the only edible portion of the plant. The heart-shaped, wide-veined leaves are concentrated with oxalic acid—they are poisonous!

Rhubarb Selection, Usage and Storage
Choose moderately thin, crisp, dark pink to red stalks. If purchased with leaves intact, avoid those with leaves that are wilted, pithy, stringy or rough-textured. Hothouse variety is normally available year-round, and the field-grown variety's peak season is from April to June.

To Prepare Rhubarb for Cooking

Remove all the leaves, rinse the stalks and pat dry. Trim the ends of stalks and cut into 1-inch pieces. Now it is ready to cook by adding a little water and sugar. It will cook down quickly into a syrupy liquid. The tartness will be determined by the amount of sugar used.

Using Nonreactive Pans

Since rhubarb is fairly acidic, you'll want to use nonreactive cookware, bakeware and storage containers. Nonreactive means that the acidity in the food has no chemical reaction with the surface of the pan or storage container. Clay, plastic, glass, stainless steel and enamel are examples of nonreactive surfaces. In addition, nonstick and anodized aluminum are considered nonreactive. Uncoated aluminum, uncoated copper and unseasoned cast iron surfaces are reactive, and may give acidic foods an "off" flavor or discolor them if they are in contact with the reactive surface for a long time. If your aluminum and copper surfaces are coated, and if your cast iron is well seasoned, you should have no troubles.

To Store

Remove leaves and trim the ends of stalks. Wash and pat dry; store in a food plastic bag 3–5 days in the refrigerator crisper drawer.

To Freeze

Cut the cleaned rhubarb stalks into 1-inch pieces; place in a food plastic bag; seal. Frozen rhubarb will keep up to a year. One pound of raw fresh rhubarb will yield about 3 cups chopped raw, or 2 cups chopped cooked.

Planting Rhubarb

You can start rhubarb from seed, but the process is long, and often does not produce a true type of rhubarb. If you can get three root divisions from a friend, that would be plenty for one family.

After fertilizing (see below), plant your divisions or crowns in the early spring in well-prepared, weed-free soil with a pH of 6.0 to 6.8. Set plants in the ground so that the buds lie about an inch below soil surface. You will find this year's buds in a protective layer of last year's leaves. Place plants in the ground with buds topmost. Set plants 3 feet apart in the row; space rows 5 feet apart. Cover buds and tamp down firmly. Do not leave air pockets around the buds, as this will cause the buds to dry out.

Fertilizing

Work ¼ cup of 10-10-10 fertilizer per plant in the soil before planting. The following spring and thereafter, apply 1 cup 10-10-10 per plant in a circle around the plant. Well-rotted animal manure is a good choice for fertilizer.

Weeding

Keep the area weed-free by hand, and allow good air circulation.

Harvesting

Do not harvest rhubarb the first year. Harvest a few stalks per plant the second year. In the third year, harvest all stalks that are an inch and larger in diameter for a period of 6–8 weeks. Leave the smaller stalks to make food for the crown and next year's crop. Harvest season usually starts in May and extends to early June. Some harvesting in the fall is acceptable. Harvest the rhubarb by snapping the stalk off at the base. Seeds stalks that appear should be snapped off. Divide plants after 3–5 years to maintain petiole or stalk size and production. Pick a spot you want to keep for a long time; rhubarb will last for years. You don't want to have to move it often, as it takes two years to become fully established before you can harvest.

Cobblers
Crumbles
Crunches
Crisps

PEACHY RHUBARB COBBLER

Fresh or frozen peaches may be used in this tasty cobbler.

Topping
1 cup all-purpose flour
2 tablespoons granulated sugar
2 teaspoons baking powder
⅛ teaspoon salt
¼ cup cold butter
⅓ cup whole milk
3 tablespoons peach
   all-fruit spread

Filling
¾ cup granulated sugar
2 tablespoons cornstarch
½ teaspoon ground cinnamon
⅛ teaspoon ground nutmeg
3 cups sliced peaches
3 cups rhubarb, sliced
1 teaspoon pure vanilla extract
1 tablespoon granulated sugar

Topping: Stir flour, sugar, baking powder and salt in a bowl. Cut in butter until crumbly. Stir in milk just until moistened. Knead dough on a floured surface until a ball forms. Roll ball out to a 9x8-inch rectangle. Spread with peach all-fruit. Starting at the 8-inch side, roll up jelly-roll style. Cut into 1-inch slices.

Preheat oven to 400°.
Filling: Mix sugar, cornstarch, cinnamon and nutmeg in a 3-quart saucepan. Add peaches and rhubarb; bring to a boil, stirring constantly, over medium heat. Remove from heat; stir in vanilla. Pour immediately into a greased 8-inch baking pan; top with dough; sprinkle with 1 tablespoon sugar. Bake 20–25 minutes. Serve warm. Refrigerate leftovers.

Makes 9 servings.

PEAR-RHUBARB COBBLER

Serve warm with vanilla ice cream.

Filling
1 10-ounce package sweetened frozen rhubarb, thawed
3 ripe pears, peeled, cored and cut into ½-inch cubes
2 tablespoons water
1 teaspoon pure vanilla extract
¼ cup granulated sugar*
2 tablespoons cornstarch
½ teaspoon ground cinnamon
⅛ teaspoon salt
1½ tablespoons butter, cut up

Topping
1¼ cups prepared biscuit mix
1 tablespoon granulated sugar
2 tablespoons butter, melted
½ cup milk
1 tablespoon granulated sugar

Preheat oven to 400°.
Filling: Place rhubarb, pears, water and vanilla into a mixing bowl. In a small bowl, mix sugar, cornstarch, cinnamon and salt; stir into first bowl. Pour mixture into a greased 8-inch square baking pan. Dot with butter. Cover and bake until bubbly, about 10 minutes. Remove from oven.

Topping: Mix biscuit mix and 1 tablespoon sugar in a bowl. Stir in butter and milk with a fork. Drop by spoonfuls on top of hot fruit mixture. Sprinkle with 1 tablespoon granulated sugar. Bake 15–20 minutes or until biscuit is done. Refrigerate leftovers.

*If the rhubarb you are using is unsweetened, increase sugar to ⅔ cup.

Makes 6 servings.

RHUBARB COBBLER

Serve warm in dessert bowls topped with a scoop of vanilla ice cream.

Filling
2 pounds fresh rhubarb, diced
2 cups granulated sugar
4 tablespoons butter
3 tablespoons fresh lemon juice

Crust
¼ cup granulated sugar
2 teaspoons butter
1 egg
1 cup all-purpose flour mixed with 1 tablespoon baking powder,
  1 teaspoon ground cinnamon, ½ teaspoon salt and
  ¼ teaspoon ground nutmeg
½ cup buttermilk mixed with 1 tablespoon pure vanilla extract

Preheat oven to 375°.
Generously butter a 2½-quart glass baking casserole.
Filling: Mix rhubarb, sugar, butter and lemon juice in a saucepan; cook and stir until soft, about 7 minutes. Pour into prepared casserole.

Crust: In a bowl, beat sugar and butter until creamy. Beat in egg. Slowly beat in flour mixture alternately with buttermilk mixture to a cake-like batter; pour over hot rhubarb mixture. Bake 30–35 minutes or until center is done. Refrigerate leftovers.

Makes 12 servings.

STRAWBERRY-RHUBARB COBBLER

Top this warm cobbler with strawberry ice cream.

Filling
1¼ cups granulated sugar
3 tablespoons all-purpose flour
1¼ teaspoons ground cinnamon
2 teaspoons finely shredded
   lemon rind
6 cups fresh rhubarb, diced
3 cups fresh strawberries, sliced
1 teaspoon pure vanilla extract

Topping
1½ cups all-purpose flour
3 tablespoons granulated sugar
1½ teaspoons baking powder
½ teaspoon baking soda
¼ teaspoon salt
3 tablespoons cold butter or
   margarine
1 cup buttermilk

Preheat oven to 400°.
Filling: Mix sugar, flour and cinnamon in a large bowl. Add lemon rind, rhubarb and strawberries; gently toss until coated. Drizzle top with vanilla extract. Pour mixture into a greased 13x9-inch baking dish. Bake 10 minutes.

Topping: Mix first five topping ingredients in a large bowl. Cut in butter until mixture resembles pea size. Stir in buttermilk with a fork just until a soft dough is formed. Drop dough by the tablespoonfuls on top of hot fruit mixture, creating 12 portions. Continue baking at 400° until topping is puffed and browned, about 25 minutes. Let stand 10 minutes before serving. Serve warm. Refrigerate leftovers.

Makes 12 servings.

APPLE-BERRY-RHUBARB CRUMBLE

Apples, strawberries and rhubarb in this good crumble. Serve warm or cold with a scoop of vanilla ice cream.

Filling
3 cups fresh rhubarb, cut into ½-inch pieces
1 cup apples, peeled and cubed
½ cup strawberries, sliced
1 teaspoon pure vanilla extract
⅓ cup granulated sugar
½ teaspoon ground cinnamon

Topping
½ cup all-purpose flour
1 teaspoon baking powder
¼ teaspoon salt
4 tablespoons butter or margarine
⅔ cup brown sugar, packed
⅔ cup quick-cooking oatmeal

Preheat oven to 350°.
Filling: Mix rhubarb, apples and strawberries in a bowl; spoon into a greased 8-inch square baking dish; drizzle evenly with vanilla extract. Mix granulated sugar and cinnamon; sprinkle over rhubarb mixture.

Topping: In another bowl, mix flour, baking powder and salt. Cut in butter until mixture resembles coarse crumbs. Stir in brown sugar and oatmeal; sprinkle over rhubarb mixture. Bake 40–50 minutes or until lightly browned. Refrigerate leftovers.

Makes 8 servings.

PINEAPPLE-RHUBARB CRUMBLE

A yummy treat…best served warm with a scoop of vanilla ice cream.

Filling
7 cups fresh rhubarb, cut into 1-inch pieces
1 8-ounce can crushed pineapple
1 cup brown sugar, packed
2 tablespoons cornstarch
1 teaspoon pure vanilla extract
2 teaspoons finely shredded fresh lemon peel

Topping
⅔ cup all-purpose flour
¼ cup brown sugar, packed
1 tablespoon granulated sugar
1 tablespoon chopped crystallized ginger
⅛ teaspoon salt
⅓ cup butter

Preheat oven to 350°.
Filling: Mix rhubarb, pineapple and brown sugar in a large glass bowl. Cover and let stand 1 hour. Drain, reserving juice, and add enough water to equal ⅔ cup, if needed. Stir juice and cornstarch in a small container; pour into a saucepan; cook and stir until thickened slightly. Stir in rhubarb mixture, vanilla and lemon peel. Pour fruit mixture into a buttered 2-quart square baking dish.

Topping: In another bowl, mix all topping ingredients except butter. Cut in butter with a pastry blender until crumbly. Spoon over top of fruit. Bake 55–60 minutes or until bubbly and light brown. Refrigerate leftovers.

Makes 6 servings.

APPLE-RHUBARB CRUNCH

Golden Delicious or Granny Smith apples will be delicious in this crunch.

3 cups apples, pared and sliced
2 cups fresh rhubarb, diced
½ cup granulated sugar
1 teaspoon pure vanilla extract

½ cup all-purpose flour
½ cup light brown sugar, packed
⅓ cup quick-cooking oatmeal
½ teaspoon ground cinnamon
¼ teaspoon salt
¼ cup butter or margarine

Preheat oven to 375°.
Mix apples and rhubarb in a shallow, ungreased 2-quart baking dish; sprinkle with sugar. Drizzle with vanilla extract.

In a bowl, mix flour, sugar, oatmeal, cinnamon and salt. Cut in butter until crumbly. Spoon over fruit mixture. Bake 25–35 minutes or until fruit is tender. Serve warm with sweetened whipped cream.

Makes 6 servings.

RHUBARB CRUNCH

This plain crunch is good enough for company...serve with ice cream.

1 cup all-purpose flour
¾ cups quick-cooking oatmeal
½ cup brown sugar, packed
1 teaspoon ground cinnamon
½ cup butter, melted
4 cups fresh rhubarb, diced

1 cup granulated sugar
1 tablespoon cornstarch
1 cup water
1 teaspoon pure vanilla extract

Preheat oven to 350°.
Mix flour, oatmeal, brown sugar and cinnamon in a bowl; stir in butter. Press half the mixture into an ungreased 9-inch square baking pan. Top with rhubarb.

Mix granulated sugar and cornstarch in a medium saucepan. Stir in water and vanilla until blended. Cook and stir over medium heat until thick and clear. Carefully pour over rhubarb. Sprinkle evenly with remaining crumb mixture. Bake 1 hour. Serve warm or cold. Refrigerate leftovers.

Makes 9 servings.

STRAWBERRY-RHUBARB CRUNCH

A delicious crunch…serve with whipped topping.

1 cup granulated sugar
3 tablespoons all-purpose flour
3 cups rhubarb, diced
1 cup fresh strawberries, sliced
1 teaspoon pure vanilla extract

Topping
1½ cups all-purpose flour
1 cup brown sugar, packed
1 cup butter or margarine

Preheat oven to 375°.
Mix granulated sugar and flour in a large bowl. Stir in rhubarb, strawberries and vanilla. Pour mixture into an ungreased 13x9-inch baking dish.

Topping: Mix flour and brown sugar in a bowl; cut in butter until crumbly. Sprinkle over rhubarb mixture. Bake 45 minutes. Refrigerate leftovers.

Makes 12 servings.

APPLE-RHUBARB CRISP

Apple crisp, always a favorite...now with rhubarb.

Topping
¾ cup all-purpose flour
¾ cup light brown sugar
½ cup old-fashioned oatmeal
½ teaspoon ground cinnamon
¼ teaspoon ground cloves
6 tablespoons soft butter
½ cup walnuts, finely chopped

Filling
4 cups apples, such as Golden Delicious, cut into ½-inch pieces
3 cups fresh rhubarb, cut into ½-inch pieces
3 tablespoons granulated sugar
2 teaspoons all-purpose flour
1 teaspoon pure vanilla extract

Preheat oven to 400°.
Topping: Mix first five ingredients in a bowl. Cut in butter until coarse clumps form. Stir in nuts.

Filling: Mix all filling ingredients in a large bowl until coated. Spoon into an ungreased 8x8-inch square glass baking dish. Sprinkle topping mixture over fruit. Bake 45–50 minutes or until fruit is tender and topping is crisp. Remove from oven; cool a little before serving. Refrigerate leftovers.

Makes 6 servings.

BLUEBERRY-RHUBARB CRISP

Blueberries are good in just about any dessert. Serve this crisp warm with a dollop of sweetened whipped cream.

Filling
2 tablespoons all-purpose flour
⅓ cup granulated sugar
2 cups fresh rhubarb, cut into ½-inch pieces
2 cups blueberries-
1 teaspoon pure vanilla extract

Topping
¾ cup all-purpose flour
½ cup granulated sugar
¼ cup brown sugar, packed
¾ cup cold butter, cut up
⅓ cup shelled natural pistachios, finely chopped

Preheat oven to 375°.
Filling: Mix flour and granulated sugar in a bowl. Stir in rhubarb and blueberries until coated. Spoon mixture into a greased, shallow 2-quart baking dish. Drizzle top with vanilla.

Topping: Mix flour and sugars. Cut in butter with a pastry blender until mixture resembles coarse meal. Stir in pistachios. Squeeze mixture with hands, and crumble over filling. Bake 45–50 minutes or until bubbly and top is crisp and golden. Refrigerate leftovers.

Makes 8 servings.

CHERRY-RHUBARB CRISP

All cherry fans will go for this crisp. Serve with vanilla ice cream.

Crust
1 cup quick-cooking oatmeal
1 cup light brown sugar, packed
1 cup all-purpose flour
⅛ teaspoon salt
½ cup butter

Filling
4 cups fresh rhubarb, diced
1 cup granulated sugar
1 cup water
2 tablespoons cornstarch
1 teaspoon pure vanilla extract
¼ teaspoon almond extract
1 21-ounce can cherry pie filling
½ cup walnuts, chopped

Preheat oven to 350°.
Crust: In a bowl, mix oatmeal, brown sugar, flour and salt; cut in butter until crumbs form. Press half of mixture onto bottom of an ungreased 13x9-inch baking pan.

Filling: Spread rhubarb over crust. Mix granulated sugar, water and cornstarch in a saucepan; stir until blended. Bring to a boil, stirring until thickened. Stir in extracts and pie filling; spoon mixture over rhubarb. Sprinkle with remaining crust mixture. Sprinkle top with walnuts. Bake 45–55 minutes. Serve warm. Refrigerate leftovers.

Makes 8 servings.

CRANBERRY-APPLE-RHUBARB CRISP

Fresh or frozen cranberries will work well in this sweet crisp. Serve warm with vanilla ice cream.

Topping
⅓ cup brown sugar, packed
⅓ cup quick-cooking oatmeal
3 tablespoons whole wheat flour
2 tablespoons margarine, melted

Filling
⅔ cup granulated sugar
3 tablespoons all-purpose flour
2 cups apples, sliced
2 cups rhubarb, diced
1 cup cranberries
1 teaspoon pure vanilla extract

Preheat oven to 375°.
Topping: Mix all topping ingredients in a bowl until crumbly.

Filling: In another bowl, mix sugar and all-purpose flour. Stir in apples, rhubarb and cranberries. Spoon mixture into an ungreased 2½-quart shallow baking dish. Drizzle with vanilla. Sprinkle with topping mixture. Bake about 50 minutes or until fruit is tender. Refrigerate leftovers.

Makes 8 servings.

MANDARIN-RHUBARB CRISP

Mandarin oranges and rhubarb…serve warm with vanilla ice cream.

6 cups fresh rhubarb, chopped
1½ cups granulated sugar
5 tablespoons quick-cooking tapioca
1 teaspoon pure vanilla extract

1 11-ounce can mandarin oranges, drained

1 cup brown sugar, packed
1 cup quick-cooking oatmeal
½ cup all-purpose flour
½ teaspoon salt
½ cup cold butter

Preheat oven to 350°.
Mix rhubarb, granulated sugar and tapioca in a glass bowl; let stand 15 minutes. Stir in vanilla; pour mixture into a greased 13x9-inch baking pan. Top with mandarin oranges. Mix brown sugar, oatmeal, flour and salt in a bowl; cut in butter until crumbly. Sprinkle over last layer. Bake 40 minutes or until golden brown. Refrigerate leftovers.

Makes 12 servings.

MICROWAVE RHUBARB CRISP

Serve warm with vanilla ice cream.

4 cups fresh rhubarb, cut into ½-inch pieces
½ cup granulated sugar
2 tablespoons fresh lemon juice
½ teaspoon pure vanilla extract

¾ cup brown sugar, packed
¾ cup all-purpose flour
3 tablespoons butter

Mix first four ingredients in a bowl; place mixture into an ungreased 8x8x2-inch microwave-safe glass baking dish.

In another bowl, mix brown sugar and flour; cut in butter until crumbly. Sprinkle over rhubarb mixture. Microwave on 100% power until rhubarb is tender, about 10–15 minutes, turning a quarter turn every 2 minutes. Cool slightly before serving. Refrigerate leftovers.

Microwave ovens will vary, so be watchful before the end of the cooking period.

Makes 6 servings.

QUICK STRAWBERRY-RHUBARB CRISP

Serve this quick crisp with vanilla ice cream.

1 pound fresh rhubarb, cut into 1-inch pieces (about 4 cups)
¼ cup water
⅔ cup granulated sugar mixed in a bowl
   with 3 tablespoons cornstarch
½ pint fresh strawberries, sliced
1 teaspoon pure vanilla extract

3 cups prepared granola
2 tablespoons butter, melted
½ teaspoon ground cinnamon

Grease a 9x7-inch baking pan.
In a saucepan, bring rhubarb and water to a boil over medium heat; cover and cook, stirring occasionally until rhubarb is tender, about 5 minutes. Quickly stir sugar and cornstarch mixture into hot cooked rhubarb; cook and stir until mixture boils and thickens. Stir in strawberries and vanilla; cook 1 minute. Remove from heat; stir in more sugar if not sweet enough.

Mix granola, butter and cinnamon in a bowl; place half the mixture into prepared pan. Toast in a toaster oven about 2 minutes, or until slightly browned. Spoon hot rhubarb mixture over granola. Sprinkle with remaining granola. Place in toaster oven and toast until topping begins to brown, about 3 minutes. Serve warm. Refrigerate leftovers.

Makes 6 servings.

RHUBARB CRISP

A scoop of vanilla ice cream will complete this tasty dessert.

Filling
4 cups fresh rhubarb, cut into ¾-inch pieces (about 1 pound)
1 cup granulated sugar
¼ cup all-purpose flour
1 teaspoon ground cinnamon
1 teaspoon pure vanilla extract

Topping
1 cup all-purpose flour
1 cup brown sugar, packed
½ cup old-fashioned oatmeal
½ cup butter, melted and cooled

Preheat oven to 375°.
Filling: Mix first four ingredients in a large bowl until coated. Spoon into four 4-inch greased individual baking dishes. Drizzle equally with vanilla extract.

Topping: In another bowl, mix all topping ingredients until crumbly. Sprinkle over filling. Bake 35–45 minutes or until rhubarb is tender and topping is golden brown. Serve warm. Refrigerate leftovers.

Makes 4 servings.

STRAWBERRY-RHUBARB CRISP

Spring favorites in a crisp.

3 cups fresh rhubarb, cut into 1-inch pieces
1 pint fresh strawberries, halved
½ cup granulated sugar
1 teaspoon pure vanilla extract

¼ cup all-purpose flour
¾ cup quick-cooking oatmeal
¾ cup brown sugar, packed
⅓ cup butter or margarine, melted

Preheat oven to 350°.
Mix rhubarb, strawberries and granulated sugar in a bowl; pour into an ungreased 9-inch square baking dish. Drizzle with vanilla extract.

Mix remaining ingredients in a bowl until crumbly; sprinkle over rhubarb mixture. Bake about 40 minutes or until rhubarb is tender. Serve warm topped with sweetened whipped cream. Refrigerate leftovers.

Makes 8 servings.

Cakes
Coffee Cakes

APPLE-RHUBARB DUMP CAKE

Pretty easy...good too.

2 cups fresh rhubarb, coarsely chopped
2 cups apple pie filling
1 cup granulated sugar mixed with 1 (3-ounce) package
strawberry-flavored dry gelatin dessert mix
1 package (18.25-ounce) white cake mix
1½ cups water
½ cup butter, cut into small pieces

Preheat oven to 350°.
Spread rhubarb into a greased 13x9-inch baking pan. Top evenly with apple pie filling. Sprinkle with sugar mixture. Sprinkle with dry cake mix. Sprinkle evenly with water. Dot with butter. Bake 45–50 minutes. Serve warm with vanilla ice cream. Refrigerate leftovers.

Makes 12 servings.

APPLESAUCE-RHUBARB CAKE

Plain, but tasty…easy to prepare.

3 eggs
1¼ cups granulated sugar
¼ teaspoon salt
1 teaspoon pure vanilla extract
2 cups all-purpose flour, mixed with 1 teaspoon baking soda
  and 2 teaspoons ground cinnamon
1 cup plain applesauce
3 cups fresh rhubarb, cut into ½-inch pieces
½ cup walnuts, chopped
powdered sugar

Preheat oven to 350°.
Grease a 13x9-inch baking pan. Beat eggs, sugar, salt and vanilla in a
large bowl. Stir in flour mixture. Stir in applesauce, rhubarb and walnuts until
blended. Pour batter into prepared pan. Bake 1 hour. Remove from oven;
cool. Dust with powdered sugar. Serve warm or cold. Refrigerate leftovers.

Makes 16 servings.

CHOCOLATE CHIP RHUBARB CAKE

This cake is for all you chocolate lovers!

Cake
1½ cups brown sugar, packed
½ cup shortening
1 egg
1 teaspoon pure vanilla extract
2 cups all-purpose flour
1 teaspoon baking soda
½ teaspoon salt
1 cup buttermilk
1¾ cups fresh rhubarb, chopped
½ cup semi-sweet chocolate chips

Topping
½ cup brown sugar, packed
½ cup walnuts, chopped
½ cup semi-sweet chocolate chips
1 teaspoon ground cinnamon

Preheat oven to 350°.
Cake: Beat brown sugar and shortening in a mixing bowl until creamy. Beat in egg and vanilla. In another bowl, mix flour, soda and salt; beat into creamed mixture alternately with buttermilk. Stir in rhubarb and chocolate chips. Pour batter into a greased 13x9-inch baking pan.

Topping: Mix all topping ingredients in a bowl; sprinkle over batter. Bake 45 minutes. Serve warm or cold. Refrigerate leftovers.

Makes 12 servings.

CHOCOLATE RHUBARB CAKE

This one's for chocolate lovers.

½ cup butter, no substitute
½ cup corn oil
1¾ cups granulated sugar
2 eggs
2 teaspoons pure vanilla extract
½ cup buttermilk

2½ cups all-purpose flour
4 tablespoons unsweetened cocoa powder
1 teaspoon baking soda
1 teaspoon baking powder
½ teaspoon ground cinnamon
½ teaspoon salt

2 cups fresh rhubarb, diced
½ cup miniature chocolate chips, optional
1 cup chopped nuts, optional

Preheat oven to 325°.
Grease and flour a 13x9-inch baking pan.
Beat butter, oil and sugar in a bowl. Add eggs, vanilla and buttermilk; mix well.

In another bowl, mix flour, cocoa, baking soda, baking powder, cinnamon, and salt; stir into creamed mixture.

Stir in rhubarb, chocolate chips and nuts. Spread batter into prepared pan. Bake 40–45 minutes or until a wooden pick inserted in center comes out clean. Cool on a rack. Frost with your favorite chocolate frosting. Serve at room temperature. Refrigerate leftovers.

Makes 12 servings.

COCONUT-TOPPED RHUBARB CAKE

Spicy coconut and pecans top this rhubarb cake.

Cake
1½ cups brown sugar, packed
½ cup solid margarine
1 egg
1 teaspoon pure vanilla extract
2¼ cups all-purpose flour
1 teaspoon baking soda
1 teaspoon ground cinnamon
¼ teaspoon ground cloves
⅛ teaspoon ground ginger
1 cup buttermilk
2 cups fresh rhubarb, finely chopped

Topping
⅔ cup sweetened flaked coconut
½ cup pecans, chopped
½ cup granulated sugar
½ teaspoon ground cinnamon

Preheat oven to 350°.
Cake: Beat brown sugar and margarine in a bowl until creamy. Beat in egg and vanilla. In another bowl, mix flour, soda, cinnamon, cloves and ginger; beat into creamed mixture alternately with buttermilk. Stir in rhubarb; pour into a greased 13x9-inch baking pan.

Topping: Mix all topping ingredients in a bowl; sprinkle over batter. Bake about 40 minutes or until a wooden pick inserted in center comes out clean. Serve warm or cold. Refrigerate leftovers.

Makes 12 servings.

CREAM AND RHUBARB CAKE

Good served cold, too…top with whipped topping and sprinkle with a pinch of ground cinnamon.

1 package (18.25-ounce) yellow cake mix with pudding
1 cup water
⅓ cup corn oil
3 eggs
1 teaspoon pure vanilla extract

4 cups fresh rhubarb, sliced
1 cup granulated sugar
2 cups heavy cream

Preheat oven to 350°.
Grease and flour 13x9-inch baking pan. In a large bowl, beat cake mix, water, corn oil, eggs and vanilla on low speed until moistened. Beat 2 minutes on high speed. Pour batter into prepared pan.

Top batter with rhubarb. Sprinkle with sugar. Pour cream over top. Bake 1¼–1½ hours or until a wooden pick inserted in center comes out clean. Remove from oven; cool slightly before serving. Store in refrigerator.

Makes 12 servings.

KIKI'S EASY RHUBARB CAKE

My friend, Grandma KiKi, resides in Blaine, Minnesota, and was happy to share her old-fashioned rhubarb cake recipe.

1½ cups brown sugar, packed
¼ cup granulated sugar
¼ cup solid shortening
¼ cup butter
1 egg
1 teaspoon pure vanilla extract
2 cups all-purpose flour
1 teaspoon baking soda
1 cup buttermilk
1½ cups fresh rhubarb, chopped

Topping
⅓ cup granulated sugar mixed with 1 teaspoon ground cinnamon

Preheat oven to 350°.
In a large bowl, beat brown sugar and granulated sugar with shortening and butter until creamy. Beat in egg and vanilla. Mix flour and baking soda in another bowl; stir into creamed mixture alternately with buttermilk. Spread half the batter into a greased 13x9-inch baking pan. Spoon rhubarb evenly over top. Top with remaining batter. Sprinkle with topping mixture. Bake 50 minutes. Serve with vanilla ice cream.

Makes 12 servings.

LOLA'S RHUBARB CAKE

Lola loves cooking with rhubarb…this is one of her favorite desserts.

4 cups fresh rhubarb, cut into small pieces
1 cup granulated sugar
1 3-ounce package strawberry gelatin dessert mix
1 package (18.25-ounce) white or yellow cake mix

Preheat oven to 350°.
Sprinkle rhubarb into a buttered 13x9-inch baking pan. Sprinkle sugar and dry gelatin mix over top. Prepare cake mix as directed on package; pour batter over top. Bake 30–35 minutes or until a wooden pick inserted in center of cake portion tests done. While warm, carefully turn upside down on a large cookie sheet. Serve with vanilla ice cream or whipped topping. Refrigerate leftovers.

Makes 12 servings.

RASPBERRY GELATIN RHUBARB CAKE

A dump cake dessert.

4 cups fresh rhubarb, coarsely chopped
¾ cup granulated sugar
1 3-ounce package raspberry-flavored gelatin dessert mix
1 package (18.25-ounce) yellow cake mix
½ cup butter, melted
1 cup water*

Preheat oven to 350°.
Spread rhubarb evenly into an ungreased 13x9-inch baking pan. Sprinkle with sugar, then sprinkle with dry raspberry gelatin mix. Sprinkle with dry cake mix. Pour butter evenly over top of cake mix layer, then pour water over top. Bake 45–50 minutes. Serve at room temperature. Refrigerate leftovers.

Makes 12 servings.

*If using frozen rhubarb, reduce water to ½ cup.

RHUBARB CAKE WITH SAUCE

For an extra taste treat, serve a scoop of vanilla ice cream on the side.

Cake
1½ cups brown sugar, packed
¼ cup granulated sugar
½ cup butter, softened
1 egg
1 teaspoon pure vanilla extract
2½ cups all-purpose flour
1 teaspoon baking soda
½ teaspoon salt
1 cup buttermilk
2 cups rhubarb, coarsely chopped
2 tablespoons granulated sugar
½ teaspoon ground cinnamon

Sauce
2 cups fresh rhubarb, cut into
  1-inch pieces
⅔ cup granulated sugar
¼ teaspoon ground cinnamon
½ teaspoon pure vanilla extract
4 tablespoons water

Preheat oven to 350°.
Cake: Beat brown sugar, ¼ cup granulated sugar and butter in a large bowl. Beat in egg and vanilla. In another bowl, mix flour, soda and salt; beat into creamed mixture alternately with buttermilk. Spread two-thirds of batter into a greased and floured 13x9-inch baking pan. Spoon rhubarb over batter. Top with remaining batter. In a cup, mix 2 tablespoons granulated sugar and cinnamon; sprinkle over batter. Bake 40–45 minutes, until cake is golden brown. Remove from oven; cool completely.

Sauce: Bring all sauce ingredients to a boil in a saucepan. Reduce heat; cook, stirring often until rhubarb is tender. Cool. Spoon over cake when serving. Refrigerate sauce and cake leftovers.

Makes 12 servings.

RHUBARB CUSTARD CAKE

Serve this custard cake topped with sweetened whipped cream.

1 package (18.25-ounce) yellow cake mix
4 cups fresh rhubarb, chopped
1 teaspoon pure vanilla extract
1 cup granulated sugar
1 cup whipping cream

Preheat oven to 350°.
Prepare cake mix according to package directions. Pour batter into a greased 13x9-inch baking pan. Sprinkle with rhubarb; drizzle with vanilla. Sprinkle evenly with sugar. Slowly pour cream on top. Bake 40–45 minutes or until golden brown. Cool a few minutes before serving. Refrigerate leftovers.

Makes 12 servings.

RHUBARB LOAF CAKE

Serve warm, topped with sweetened whipped cream.

¼ cup butter, softened
1½ cups brown sugar, packed
1 egg
1 teaspoon pure vanilla extract
1½ cups all-purpose flour
1 teaspoon baking powder
⅛ teaspoon salt
1 cup dairy sour cream
4 cups fresh rhubarb, cut into ½-inch pieces

⅓ cup granulated sugar
½ teaspoon freshly grated nutmeg

Preheat oven to 375°.
Line a greased 8x5-inch loaf pan with parchment paper.
Beat butter and brown sugar in a bowl until creamy. Beat in egg and vanilla.
In another bowl, mix flour, baking powder and salt. Stir into creamed
mixture alternately with sour cream. Stir in rhubarb. Pour mixture into pre-
pared pan.

Mix granulated sugar with grated nutmeg; sprinkle over batter. Bake 40
minutes or until a wooden pick inserted in center comes out clean. Cool in
pan 30 minutes; remove from pan to a cooling rack. Refrigerate leftovers.

Makes 12 servings.

RHUBARB PUDDING CAKE

A quick dessert to prepare for friends to enjoy.

Cake
1½ cups granulated sugar
1¼ cups all-purpose flour
3½ teaspoons baking powder
½ teaspoon salt
2 tablespoons shortening
1 egg
½ cup milk
1 teaspoon pure vanilla extract

Topping
3 cups fresh rhubarb, diced
1 cup granulated sugar
2 cups boiling water

Preheat oven to 400°.
Cake: Stir first five ingredients in a bowl until well mixed. Stir in remaining cake ingredients; mix well. Pour batter into a generously greased 13x9-inch baking pan.

Topping: Mix all topping ingredients in a bowl; pour over batter. Do not stir. Bake about 25–35 minutes or until cake is golden brown. Serve warm or cold. Refrigerate leftovers.

Makes 12 servings.

RHUBARB REFRIGERATOR CAKE

This is more dessert-like than cake. Serve in small portions…very rich.

1 cup fresh rhubarb, chopped

1 14-ounce can sweetened condensed milk (not evaporated milk)
¼ cup fresh lemon juice
½ teaspoon pure vanilla extract
28 vanilla wafers

Cook chopped rhubarb with a little water in a saucepan until tender. Set aside.

Stir sweetened condensed milk, lemon juice and vanilla in a bowl; mix well. Stir in cooked rhubarb. Line a narrow 7x5-inch baking pan with waxed paper. Fill with alternate layers of rhubarb mixture and wafers, ending with layer of wafers. Freeze. Remove from pan to a serving platter; remove waxed paper. Cut into slices and serve. Freeze leftovers.

Makes 8 servings.

RHUBARB SKILLET CAKE

Serve warm with vanilla ice cream.

7 tablespoons butter
4 tablespoons light brown sugar, packed
1½ pounds fresh rhubarb, cut into1-inch pieces

Dry Ingredients
1 cup all-purpose flour
1 cup yellow cornmeal
¾ cup granulated sugar
1 teaspoon baking powder
½ teaspoon baking soda
1 teaspoon ground ginger
½ teaspoon ground cinnamon

Wet Ingredients
2 large eggs
½ cup buttermilk
2 tablespoons molasses
1 teaspoon pure vanilla extract

Preheat oven to 400°.
Melt butter in a 10-inch non-stick ovenproof skillet; reserve 4 teaspoons and set aside. Stir brown sugar into skillet until dissolved. Add rhubarb; stir and cook 10 minutes.

Mix dry ingredients in a bowl. In another bowl, whisk together wet ingredients and reserved butter. Add mixture to dry ingredients, and stir just enough to combine. Pour batter over ingredients in prepared skillet. Bake 20–24 minutes or until a wooden pick inserted in center comes out clean. Immediately place a serving plate over skillet; quickly and carefully invert cake onto plate. Spoon any stuck rhubarb in skillet over cake. Refrigerate leftovers.

Makes 6 servings.

RHUBARB-STRAWBERRY ANGEL CAKE

A delicious cake...use cream cheese in place of ricotta if you prefer.

Filling
2 cups fresh rhubarb, thinly sliced
½ cup granulated sugar
2 tablespoons fresh orange juice
1 teaspoon finely shredded orange peel
1 teaspoon pure vanilla extract
2 cups fresh strawberries, sliced and divided

1 round angel food cake, purchased or homemade

Frosting
1 15-ounce container ricotta cheese
¼ cup powdered sugar
2 cups nondairy frozen whipped topping, thawed

Filling: Mix rhubarb, granulated sugar, orange juice, orange peel and vanilla extract in a saucepan. Cook over medium heat, stirring often, until rhubarb is tender, about 8 minutes. Remove from heat. Cool slightly, then stir in 1½ cups sliced strawberries. Chill 1 hour.

Frosting: Beat cheese and powdered sugar in a large bowl until fluffy. Fold in whipped topping.

Cut angel food cake horizontally to make 3 layers. Spread chilled rhubarb mixture between layers. Frost top and sides with cheese mixture. Top with ½ cup sliced strawberries. Refrigerate.

Makes 10 servings.

RHUBARB UPSIDE-DOWN CAKE

Best served warm, but good cold too...with whipped topping!

⅔ cup boiling water
½ cup quick-cooking oatmeal
2 tablespoons butter, melted
⅓ cup granulated sugar

2 cups fresh rhubarb, diced

⅔ cup granulated sugar
½ cup brown sugar, packed
¼ cup corn oil
1 teaspoon pure vanilla extract
1 egg

1 cup all-purpose flour mixed
in a bowl with:
1 teaspoon baking powder
¼ teaspoon baking soda
½ teaspoon ground cinnamon
¼ teaspoon salt

Preheat oven to 350°.
Pour boiling water over oatmeal in a bowl; cover and let stand 20 minutes.

Stir melted butter and granulated sugar in an 8-inch square baking pan.
Sprinkle with rhubarb.

In a large bowl, beat granulated sugar, brown sugar, corn oil, vanilla and egg.
Add oat mixture; beat well. Add flour mixture; beat just to combine. Carefully
pour mixture over rhubarb. Bake about 50 minutes or until a wooden pick
inserted in center comes out clean. Cool in pan on a rack 5 minutes. Run a
knife along sides of pan to loosen cake. Carefully invert cake onto a cake
plate. Refrigerate leftovers.

Makes 8 servings.

RHUBARB WALNUT CAKE

Serve warm with vanilla ice cream, or cool with whipped topping.

Cake
1½ cups brown sugar, packed
½ cup butter, softened
1 egg
1 teaspoon pure vanilla extract
2 cups all-purpose flour
1 teaspoon salt
1 teaspoon baking soda
1 cup buttermilk
2 cups fresh rhubarb, finely chopped
1 cup walnuts, chopped

Topping
¾ cups brown sugar
1 tablespoon ground cinnamon
2 tablespoons all-purpose flour
3 tablespoons butter, cut up

Preheat oven to 350°.
Cake: Beat brown sugar and butter in a bowl. Beat in egg and vanilla. In another bowl, mix flour, salt and soda; beat into creamed mixture alternately with buttermilk. Stir in rhubarb and walnuts. Pour batter into a greased 13x9-inch baking pan.

Topping: Mix first three ingredients in a small bowl; cut in butter until crumbly; sprinkle over batter. Bake 45–50 minutes. Refrigerate leftovers.

Makes 12 servings.

SOUR CREAM RHUBARB CRUMB CAKE

Cinnamon aroma fills the kitchen while this rhubarb cake bakes!

Cake
1½ cups granulated sugar
¾ cup butter, softened
3 eggs
1½ teaspoons pure vanilla extract
2¾ cups all-purpose flour
2 teaspoons baking powder
1 teaspoon baking soda
¾ teaspoon salt
1 cup dairy sour cream
3 cups diced fresh rhubarb tossed with ¼ cup
  all-purpose flour in a bowl

Topping
½ cup brown sugar, packed
¼ cup all-purpose flour
1 teaspoon ground cinnamon
¼ cup cold butter, cut up

Preheat oven to 350°.
Cake: Beat sugar and butter in a large bowl on medium speed until blended.
Add eggs and vanilla; beat until creamy. Mix flour, baking powder, baking
soda and salt in a bowl. Add to creamed mixture alternately with sour cream,
mixing well. Stir in rhubarb. Spread into a greased 13x9-inch baking pan.

Topping: Mix brown sugar, flour and cinnamon in a bowl; cut in butter until
crumbly. Sprinkle over batter. Bake 45–55 minutes or until a wooden pick
inserted in center comes out clean. Serve warm or at room temperature.
Refrigerate leftovers.

Makes 15 servings.

STRAWBERRY-RHUBARB DUMP CAKE

Serve this cake in dessert bowls like a cobbler…top with whipped cream.

4 cups fresh strawberries, sliced
4 cups fresh rhubarb, coarsely chopped
1 cup granulated sugar
1 6-ounce package strawberry-flavored gelatin dessert mix
1 package (18.25-ounce) white cake mix
½ cup butter, melted
½ cup water mixed with 1 teaspoon pure vanilla extract

Preheat oven to 350°.
Mix strawberries and rhubarb in a large bowl; pour evenly into a greased 13x9-inch baking pan. Sprinkle with sugar, then with dry gelatin. Sprinkle evenly with dry cake mix. Drizzle with melted butter and then with water mixture. Bake 40–50 minutes. Serve warm. Refrigerate leftovers.

Makes 12 servings.

ALMOND RHUBARB COFFEE CAKE

Almond and rhubarb coffee cake…a delightful breakfast treat.

1½ cups brown sugar, packed
⅔ cup corn oil
1 egg
1 teaspoon pure vanilla extract

2½ cups all-purpose flour
1 teaspoon baking soda
1 teaspoon salt
1 cup milk
1½ cups rhubarb, chopped
½ cup sliced almonds

⅓ cup granulated sugar
1 tablespoon butter, melted
¼ cup sliced almonds

Preheat oven to 350°.
Grease two 9-inch round baking cake pans. In a large bowl, beat brown sugar, corn oil, egg and vanilla until smooth. In another bowl, mix flour, baking soda and salt. Add to first mixture alternately with milk. Beat until smooth. Stir in rhubarb and almonds by hand. Pour batter into prepared pans. Mix granulated sugar, melted butter and almonds in a bowl. Sprinkle over batter. Bake 30–35 minutes or until a wooden pick inserted in center comes out clean. Cool. Refrigerate leftovers.

Makes 2 round cakes.

APPLESAUCE-RHUBARB COFFEE CAKE

Applesauce and yogurt make this coffee cake moist.

2 cups cake flour
1 teaspoon baking powder
1 teaspoon baking soda
½ teaspoon salt

1 cup light brown sugar, packed
¼ cup frozen egg substitute, thawed, or 1 egg
1 cup plain yogurt
½ cup applesauce
1 teaspoon pure vanilla extract
3 cups fresh rhubarb, coarsely chopped

2 tablespoons light brown sugar, packed

Preheat oven to 350°.
Spray a 9x9-inch square baking pan with non-stick cooking vegetable spray. Sift flour, baking powder, baking soda and salt into a large bowl.

Stir in 1 cup brown sugar. Stir in egg substitute, yogurt, applesauce and vanilla just until blended. Stir in rhubarb just until mixed. Pour batter into prepared pan. Sprinkle with 2 tablespoons brown sugar. Bake 30–35 minutes or until a wooden pick inserted in center comes out clean. Serve warm. Refrigerate leftovers.

Makes 9 servings.

RAISIN-RHUBARB COFFEE CAKE

Use dark raisins in place of golden raisins if desired...both are good.

½ cup butter, softened
1½ cups brown sugar, packed
1 egg
2 cups all-purpose flour
1 teaspoon baking soda
½ teaspoon salt
1 cup sour cream
1 teaspoon pure vanilla extract
2½ cups fresh rhubarb, cut into chunks
½ cup golden raisins

Topping
½ cup granulated sugar
½ cup pecans, chopped
1 teaspoon ground cinnamon
1 tablespoon melted butter

Preheat oven to 350°.
In a bowl, beat butter and brown sugar until fluffy. Beat in egg.

In another bowl, mix flour, soda and salt; beat alternately with sour cream
into first creamy mixture, until blended. Stir in vanilla, rhubarb and raisins.
Spread into a greased and floured 13x9-inch baking pan.

Mix all topping ingredients in a bowl; sprinkle over top. Bake 40–50 minutes.
Cool slightly before cutting. Refrigerate leftovers.

Makes 12 servings.

SOUR CREAM RHUBARB COFFEE CAKE

A good choice for a late weekend breakfast.

½ cup butter, softened
1½ cups granulated sugar
2 eggs
1 cup dairy sour cream
1 teaspoon pure vanilla extract

2 cups all-purpose flour
1 teaspoon baking soda
⅛ teaspoon salt
2 cups rhubarb, finely chopped

Topping
½ cup brown sugar, packed
1 tablespoon all-purpose flour
1 teaspoon ground cinnamon
1 tablespoon butter, softened

Preheat oven to 350°.
Grease a 13x9-inch square baking pan.

Beat butter and sugar in a bowl until smooth. Beat in eggs, one at a time.
Stir in sour cream and vanilla. In another bowl, mix flour, baking soda and
salt; fold into first creamy mixture. Stir in rhubarb.

Mix all topping ingredients in a bowl until crumbly; sprinkle over top. Bake
30–40 minutes. Serve warm. Refrigerate leftovers.

Makes 8 servings.

59

STRAWBERRY-RHUBARB COFFEE CAKE

Strawberry and rhubarb…a juicy affair.

Filling
**3 cups rhubarb, sliced into
    1-inch pieces
1 quart fresh strawberries,
    cleaned and mashed
2 tablespoons fresh lemon juice
1 cup granulated sugar, mixed
    with ⅓ cup cornstarch in a bowl**

Topping
**Mix in a bowl until crumbly:
¼ cup butter, cut up
¾ cup all-purpose flour
¾ cup granulated sugar**

Batter
**3 cups all-purpose flour
1 cup granulated sugar
1 teaspoon baking powder
1 teaspoon baking soda
½ teaspoon salt
1 cup butter, cut up
1½ cups buttermilk
2 eggs
1 teaspoon pure vanilla extract**

Preheat oven to 350°.
Grease a 13x9-inch square baking pan.
Filling: Cover and cook rhubarb, strawberries and lemon juice in a large
saucepan over medium heat 5 minutes. Stir in sugar-cornstarch mixture; bring
to a boil, stirring constantly until thickened. Remove from heat. Set aside.

Batter: In a large bowl, mix flour, sugar, baking powder, baking soda and salt.
Cut in butter until coarse crumbs form. In another bowl, beat buttermilk, eggs
and vanilla; stir into crumb mixture. Spread half the batter evenly into prepared
pan. Spread filling on top. Drop remaining crumb batter by tablespoonfuls over
filling. Sprinkle topping mixture over top. Bake 40–50 minutes. Cool in pan.
Cut into squares. Refrigerate leftovers.

Makes 16 servings.

Strudels
Bars
Squares
Cookies

PLAIN RHUBARB STRUDEL

Just plain good.

Filling
4 cups fresh rhubarb,
   cut into ½-inch pieces
1 cup granulated sugar
2 tablespoons quick-cooking tapioca
1 teaspoon grated fresh lemon rind
1 teaspoon pure vanilla extract

Pastry
6 sheets phyllo pastry
½ cup butter, melted
⅓ cup fine unflavored
   bread crumbs

powdered sugar

Preheat oven to 400°.
Filling: Mix all filling ingredients in a large bowl; toss and set aside.

Pastry: Place 1 phyllo sheet on a clean, damp kitchen tea towel; keep the remaining dough covered with another damp, clean towel.
Brush the 1 sheet of dough with some melted butter, then sprinkle with 1 tablespoon bread crumbs. Layer remaining phyllo sheets, brushing each sheet with butter and sprinkling with remaining bread crumbs.
Starting about 2 inches from long edge of pastry, spoon rhubarb mixture lengthwise down pastry in 3-inch wide strip, leaving a 2-inch border of pastry at each short end. Roll up jelly-roll style, starting at the long edge nearest filling. Place seam side down on a greased baking sheet. Brush with melted butter. Cut 7 slits on top. Bake 30–35 minutes or until golden and crisp. Remove from oven to a rack or platter. Cool 15 minutes before slicing. Sprinkle with powdered sugar. Refrigerate leftovers.

Makes 8 servings.

RHUBARB AMARETTI STRUDEL

Amaretti cookies and rhubarb in this strudel.

1 pound fresh rhubarb, cut into ½-inch pieces

9 sheets phyllo dough, thawed if frozen
1 cup unsalted butter, melted
1 cup crushed amaretti cookies
½ cup brown sugar, packed
2 teaspoons ground cinnamon
1 teaspoon freshly grated orange zest
½ cup walnuts, chopped

Preheat oven to 375°.
Blanch rhubarb in boiling water 1½ minutes, then drain and pat dry.

Place 1 sheet of phyllo on a baking sheet the same size as the dough. Brush with butter, and sprinkle with a few cookie crumbs. (Keep remaining dough covered with a damp towel.) Layer 4 more sheets of phyllo on top of the first, brushing each with butter and sprinkling with crumbs. Layer 2 more sheets of phyllo, brushing with butter but omitting the cookie crumbs.

Place a compact row of rhubarb 2 inches from one long edge of dough. Sprinkle rhubarb with cinnamon, orange zest, walnuts and any remaining cookie crumbs. Layer 2 sheets phyllo, brushing each with butter and placing over rhubarb. Starting at the edge of the rhubarb, roll up dough jelly-roll style. Turn seam-side up and brush top and sides with butter. Place seam-side down, folding both ends under to seal; brush top with butter. Bake 40–50 minutes. Let stand a few minutes before slicing. Refrigerate leftovers.

Makes 8 servings.

RHUBARB-APPLE STRUDEL

Strudel is so easy to prepare when using the purchased phyllo dough.

Filling
2 cups rhubarb, sliced
3 apples, peeled, cored and sliced
½ cup granulated sugar
2 tablespoons freshly grated lemon zest
3 tablespoons golden raisins
½ cup water
1 teaspoon pure vanilla extract
2 tablespoons tapioca

Pastry
12 sheets phyllo dough
½ cup butter, melted
½ cup walnuts, finely chopped

Preheat oven to 375°.
Filling: Mix all ingredients, except vanilla and tapioca, in a medium saucepan. Bring to a boil, then reduce heat and simmer about 12 minutes. Stir in tapioca and vanilla. Let cool. Set aside.

Pastry: Using 6 sheets of phyllo for each strudel, spread each sheet with butter, sprinkle with nuts, and stack. Spoon half the filling along the long edge of each stack. Fold the edges over to enclose the filling, then roll up jelly-roll style. Place on a greased baking sheet. Brush the tops with butter. Cut 4 slits in each strudel with a sharp knife. Bake 25 minutes or until golden brown. Cool at least 15 minutes before slicing. Refrigerate leftovers.

Makes 12 servings.

COCONUT RHUBARB BARS

Coconut and rhubarb…a good choice for a good bar.

Filling
2 cups fresh rhubarb, cut into 1-inch pieces
2 tablespoons water
⅓ cup granulated sugar
1 tablespoon cornstarch dissolved in 2 tablespoons cold water

Crust
1 cup all-purpose flour
1 teaspoon baking powder
⅛ teaspoon salt
½ cup butter or margarine
1 egg beaten with
  1 tablespoon milk

Topping
1 cup granulated sugar
½ cup butter, softened
1 egg
1 teaspoon pure vanilla extract
2 cups grated coconut

Preheat oven to 350°.
Filling: Mix rhubarb, water and sugar in a saucepan; cook over medium heat, stirring often, until tender. Stir in cornstarch mixture until sauce is thickened and clear. Remove from heat; cool.

Crust: Stir flour, baking powder and salt in a bowl. Cut in butter until crumbly. Stir in egg mixture until blended. Pat mixture onto bottom of a greased 8-inch square baking pan. Pour cooled rhubarb over crust.

Topping: Beat sugar and butter until creamy. Beat in egg and vanilla. Stir in coconut. Spread over rhubarb. Bake 30 minutes. Cool before cutting. Refrigerate leftovers.

Makes 16 servings.

CREAMY RHUBARB CUSTARD BARS

Make these cream cheese-topped dessert bars for special people.

Crust
1½ cups all-purpose flour
½ cup granulated sugar
⅛ teaspoon salt
1 cup butter, cut into small pieces

Filling
⅓ cup all-purpose flour
1½ cups granulated sugar
1½ cups cream
3 eggs, lightly beaten
5 cups fresh rhubarb, thinly sliced
½ teaspoon pure vanilla extract

Topping
2 3-ounce packages cream
cheese, softened
½ cup granulated sugar
½ teaspoon pure vanilla extract
1 cup whipping cream, whipped

Preheat oven to 350°.
Crust: Mix flour, sugar and salt in a bowl; cut in butter until crumbly. Press mixture into a lightly greased 13x9-inch baking dish. Bake until golden brown, about 15 minutes.

Filling: Mix flour and sugar in a large bowl. Stir in cream and eggs. Stir in rhubarb and vanilla. Pour over crust. Bake 40 minutes or until set. Remove from oven; cool to room temperature.

Topping: In a bowl, beat cream cheese and sugar until smooth. Beat in vanilla. Fold in whipped cream. Spread over custard. Cover and chill before cutting. Refrigerate leftovers.

Makes 16 servings.

GLAZED RHUBARB BARS

Orange glazed rhubarb bars.

1¾ cups light brown sugar, packed
1 cup corn oil
3 eggs
2 teaspoons pure vanilla extract

2¼ cups all-purpose flour
1 cup whole wheat flour
2 teaspoons baking soda
1 teaspoon baking powder
1 teaspoon salt
2 teaspoons ground cinnamon
¾ teaspoon ground nutmeg
¼ teaspoon ground cloves
¼ teaspoon ground ginger
4 cups fresh rhubarb, cut into ¼-inch dice
¾ cup walnuts, chopped

Glaze
1½ cups powdered sugar
1 teaspoon pure vanilla extract
1 teaspoon freshly grated
   orange rind
fresh orange juice, as needed

Preheat oven to 350°.
In a large bowl, beat brown sugar, corn oil, eggs and vanilla until creamy.
In another bowl, sift flours, baking soda, baking powder, salt and spices.
Add to creamed mixture; fold in until moistened. Stir in rhubarb and walnuts. Spoon batter into a buttered 15x10x2-inch jelly roll baking pan. Bake 30–40 minutes or until firm to touch in center. Cool completely.

Glaze: Stir all glaze ingredients in a bowl, adding just enough orange juice to form a spreading consistency. Glaze and cut into bars.

Makes 36 bars.

MINNESOTA RHUBARB BARS

Rhubarb bars, a good treat to take along on a picnic...thanks Lola.

Crust
1 cup all-purpose flour
1 teaspoon baking powder
¼ teaspoon salt
¼ cup butter, cut up
1 egg
1 tablespoon milk

Filling
2 cups fresh rhubarb, cut up
1 3-ounce package strawberry-flavored gelatin

Topping
1 cup granulated sugar
½ cup all-purpose flour
¼ cup butter, cut up

Preheat oven to 350°.
Crust: Mix flour, baking powder and salt in a bowl. Cut in butter until crumbly. Stir in egg and milk. Pat mixture into a greased 9-inch square baking pan.

Filling: Spoon rhubarb evenly over crust. Sprinkle with dry strawberry gelatin.

Topping: Mix sugar and flour in a bowl; cut in butter until crumbly. Sprinkle mixture evenly over top. Bake 50 minutes. Cut into bars.

Makes 16 bars.

OATMEAL RHUBARB BARS

A bar perfect for that afternoon coffee break…recipe courtesy of Doris, Rochert, Minnesota.

Filling
2 tablespoons cornstarch dissolved in ¼ cup water
3 cups fresh rhubarb, cut up
1½ cups granulated sugar
1 teaspoon pure vanilla extract

Crust
1½ cups quick-cooking oatmeal
1½ cups all-purpose flour
1 cup brown sugar
½ teaspoon baking soda
1 cup shortening
½ cup chopped nuts

Preheat oven to 375°.
Filling: Place cornstarch mixture in a saucepan. Add remaining ingredients; cook until thick, stirring often, about 8 minutes.

Crust: Mix all ingredients in a bowl until crumbly. Pat three-quarters of the mixture in an ungreased 13x9-inch baking pan. Pour rhubarb mixture over crust. Top with remaining crumb mixture. Bake 30–35 minutes. Cool before cutting into bars. Refrigerate leftovers.

Makes 16 bars.

PECAN RHUBARB OATMEAL BARS

These spiced oat rhubarb bars are so easy to prepare.

Crust
1½ cups all-purpose flour
1½ cups quick-cooking oatmeal
1 cup light brown sugar, packed
½ teaspoon ground cinnamon
½ teaspoon salt
¾ cup butter, softened

½ cup pecans, chopped

Filling
4 cups fresh rhubarb, cut into
  1-inch pieces
6 tablespoons granulated sugar
2 tablespoons fresh orange juice
1 teaspoon pure vanilla extract
½ teaspoon freshly grated orange rind
⅛ teaspoon ground nutmeg
⅛ teaspoon salt

2 tablespoons cornstarch dissolved
  in 3 tablespoons cold water

Preheat oven to 375°.
Crust: Mix flour, oatmeal, brown sugar, cinnamon and salt in a bowl. Cut in butter until crumbly. Press two-thirds of mixture into bottom of a lightly greased 13x9-inch baking pan.

Filling: Bring all ingredients, except cornstarch mixture, to a boil in a saucepan. Reduce heat; simmer until rhubarb is tender, about 10 minutes. Stir in cornstarch mixture; cook until thickened and clear. Remove from heat; cool. Spread evenly over crust. Mix remaining crust mixture with pecans in a bowl; sprinkle over top. Bake 30–35 minutes, or until golden and the rhubarb sauce is bubbly. Cool. Cut into bars. Refrigerate leftovers.

Makes 16 servings.

RHUBARB CHEESECAKE BARS

This is a good bar to serve for that special tea.

2½ cups all-purpose flour
2 cups quick-cooking oatmeal
1 cup brown sugar, packed
1 cup butter or margarine, softened
½ teaspoon salt
½ teaspoon baking soda

3 8-ounce packages cream cheese, softened
3 eggs
¾ cup granulated sugar
1 teaspoon pure vanilla extract

2 cups fresh rhubarb, chopped

Preheat oven to 350°.
Grease a 15x10-inch jelly roll baking pan all over with shortening. Beat flour, oatmeal, brown sugar, butter, salt and baking soda in a large bowl on medium speed until crumbly. Press 4 cups of mixture into the prepared pan.

Beat remaining ingredients, except rhubarb, in a bowl until blended. Stir in rhubarb by hand. Spread over crust. Sprinkle with remaining crumb mixture, and press down lightly.

Bake 40–50 minutes or until center is set. Let stand at room temperature 15 minutes. Cover and refrigerate until chilled. Use within 48 hours. Cut into bars. Store in refrigerator.

Makes 5 dozen bars.

RHUBARB-STRAWBERRY BARS

Yummy strawberry preserves meets rhubarb in this good bar.

Filling
1 cup rhubarb, sliced
⅓ cup water
1 tablespoon granulated sugar
1 cup strawberry preserves
2 tablespoons cornstarch
1 teaspoon freshly grated orange peel
½ teaspoon pure vanilla extract

Crust
1½ cups quick-cooking oatmeal
1 cup all-purpose flour
¾ cup brown sugar, packed
2 tablespoons toasted wheat germ or ground nuts
¼ teaspoon baking soda
¾ cup butter, softened

Topping
¾ cup powdered sugar
3 tablespoons orange juice, approximately
½ teaspoon pure vanilla extract

Preheat oven to 350°.
Filling: In a saucepan, mix rhubarb, water and granulated sugar. Bring to a boil over medium heat, then reduce heat to low. Cover and cook until rhubarb is soft, about 5 minutes. Mix preserves, cornstarch and orange peel. Stir into rhubarb, stirring constantly until mixture boils and thickens. Remove from heat; stir in vanilla.

Crust: Mix all ingredients in a bowl; reserve ¾ cup crumb mixture. Press remaining mixture evenly on bottom of an ungreased 8-inch square baking pan. Bake about 20 minutes or until edges are light brown. Spread rhubarb mixture to within ¼ inch of edge of hot, partially baked crust. Crumble reserved crumb mixture over filling, and continue baking 25–30 minutes or until golden brown. Cool completely.

Topping: Stir ingredients to a drizzling consistency; drizzle over cooled bars. Cut into bars. Store leftovers in refrigerator.

Makes 16 bars.

STRAWBERRY-RHUBARB BARS

Unsweetened frozen rhubarb may be used for these moist, crumbly bars.

Filling
1½ cups rhubarb, cut into
 1-inch pieces
1½ cups fresh strawberries, sliced
1 tablespoon fresh lemon juice
½ cup granulated sugar
2 tablespoons cornstarch
½ teaspoon pure vanilla extract

Crust
1½ cups all-purpose flour
1½ cups quick-cooking oatmeal
1 cup brown sugar, packed
½ teaspoon baking soda
¼ teaspoon salt
¾ cup butter, softened

Topping
¾ cup powdered sugar
½ teaspoon pure vanilla extract
1 tablespoon milk, or as needed

Preheat oven to 350°.
Filling: Place rhubarb, strawberries and lemon juice in a 2-quart saucepan. Cover, and cook over medium heat, stirring occasionally, until tender, about 8 minutes. Mix granulated sugar and cornstarch in a small bowl. Stir into fruit mixture. Cook and stir until mixture comes to a boil. Boil 1 minute. Remove from heat. Stir in vanilla extract.

Crust: Mix flour, oatmeal, brown sugar, soda and salt in a bowl. Add butter. Beat on low speed until crumbly. Reserve 1½ cups mixture. Press remaining mixture in bottom of a greased 13x9-inch baking pan. Spread rhubarb mixture over crust; sprinkle with remaining crumb mixture. Bake 30–35 minutes or until golden brown. Cool completely.

Topping: Stir powdered sugar, vanilla extract and milk in a small bowl to a drizzle consistency. Drizzle over top of cooled bars. Cut into bars and serve. Refrigerate leftovers.

Makes 3 dozen bars.

RHUBARB MERINGUE SQUARES

Coconut meringue tops this good square.

Crust
¼ cup butter
¼ cup granulated sugar
1 egg
1 teaspoon pure vanilla extract
1¼ cups all-purpose flour,
   mixed in a bowl with:
   1 teaspoon baking powder
   and ¼ teaspoon salt

Filling
3 cups fresh rhubarb, chopped
½ cup granulated sugar
½ teaspoon ground cinnamon
2 tablespoons water
3 tablespoons cornstarch
2 tablespoons water

Topping
2 egg whites
½ cup granulated sugar
¼ cup flaked coconut

Preheat oven to 350°.
Grease an 8x8-inch square baking pan.
Crust: Beat butter and sugar in a bowl until smooth. Beat in egg and vanilla.
Stir in flour mixture until a stiff dough forms; press into bottom and ½-inch up
sides of prepared pan. Bake until firm, about 15 minutes.

Filling: In a saucepan over medium heat, mix rhubarb, sugar, cinnamon and
2 tablespoons water. Bring to a boil, then reduce heat and cook until rhubarb is
soft, about 10 minutes. In a cup mix 2 tablespoons water with cornstarch; add
to saucepan, stirring constantly, until sauce thickens. Spread over baked crust.

Topping: In a medium bowl, beat egg whites to soft peaks. Gradually beat in
sugar until stiff peaks form. Spread meringue over rhubarb layer. Sprinkle with
coconut. Bake about 10 minutes or until meringue is golden brown. Cool
completely. Cut into squares. Refrigerate leftovers.

Makes 12 squares.

SOUR CREAM RHUBARB SQUARES

Serve these squares warm or cool with cinnamon or vanilla ice cream.

1½ cups brown sugar, packed
½ cup shortening
1 egg
1 teaspoon pure vanilla extract
2 cups all-purpose flour
1 teaspoon baking soda
½ teaspoon salt
1 cup sour cream
1½ cups rhubarb, chopped

½ cup granulated sugar
½ cup walnuts, chopped
1 teaspoon ground cinnamon
1 tablespoon butter, melted and cooled

Preheat oven to 350°.
Grease and flour a 13x9-inch baking pan. In a bowl, beat brown sugar and shortening until fluffy; beat in egg and vanilla. In another bowl, mix flour, soda and salt. Add flour mixture to first bowl, alternately with sour cream. Stir in rhubarb. Pour mixture into prepared pan.

Mix granulated sugar, walnuts, cinnamon and butter in a bowl until crumbly; sprinkle over mixture in pan. Bake 45–50 minutes. Cut into squares.

Makes 20 squares.

STREUSEL RHUBARB SQUARES

Fresh or frozen rhubarb may be used, but do not thaw if using frozen.

Crust
1 cup all-purpose flour
⅓ cup powdered sugar
⅓ cup butter, no substitution

Topping
¾ cup all-purpose flour
½ cup granulated sugar
¼ teaspoon ground cinnamon
⅓ cup butter, no substitution

Filling
1¼ cups granulated sugar
¼ cup all-purpose flour
½ teaspoon salt
¼ teaspoon ground cinnamon
1 teaspoon pure vanilla extract
2 eggs, slightly beaten
3 cups rhubarb, cut into ½-inch pieces

Preheat oven to 350°.
Crust: Mix flour and sugar in a bowl; cut in butter. Press into an ungreased 9-inch square baking pan. Bake 15 minutes; cool.

Filling: Mix sugar, flour, salt, cinnamon, vanilla, eggs and rhubarb in a bowl. Pour over cooled crust.

Topping: Mix flour, sugar and cinnamon in another bowl; cut in butter until crumbly. Sprinkle over filling. Bake 45–55 minutes. Cut squares the size desired. Refrigerate leftovers.

Makes 16 squares.

RHUBARB COOKIES

Use a pinch of ground ginger if preferred to crystallized ginger.

¼ pound real butter, softened
1 cup light brown sugar, packed
1 egg
1 cup cooked rhubarb, drained

2 cups all-purpose flour
¼ teaspoon salt
1 teaspoon baking soda
1 teaspoon ground cinnamon
½ teaspoon grated nutmeg
¼ teaspoon ground cloves
2 tablespoons crystallized ginger, finely chopped
½ cup walnuts, chopped
1 cup raisins

Preheat oven to 350°.
In a bowl, beat butter and sugar until creamy. Beat in egg. Stir in rhubarb.

In another bowl, mix flour, salt, baking soda, cinnamon, nutmeg and cloves; stir into rhubarb mixture until blended. Fold in ginger, walnuts and raisins. Drop batter by tablespoonfuls onto greased baking sheets, about 1¼ inches apart. Bake about 12 minutes or until lightly browned. Cool on a rack.

Makes 2 dozen cookies.

RHUBARB PINWHEEL COOKIES

Rhubarb-strawberry pinwheel cookies...yum!

Filling
1 cup rhubarb, cut into ¼-inch pieces
½ cup fresh strawberries, sliced
½ cup granulated sugar
¼ cup cold water
2 tablespoons cornstarch,
    mixed with 2 tablespoons
    cold water

Dough
1 cup butter, softened
1 cup brown sugar, packed
1 cup granulated sugar
2 eggs
1 teaspoon pure vanilla extract
4 cups all-purpose flour, mixed
    with 1 teaspoon baking soda
    and ½ teaspoon salt

Filling: Stir rhubarb, strawberries, granulated sugar and water in a saucepan. Cover and cook until rhubarb is tender, about 5 minutes. Stir in cornstarch mixture. Cook and stir until thick and bubbly. Remove from heat; cool.

Dough: Beat butter in a large bowl until fluffy. Add brown sugar and granulated sugar; continue to beat until light and fluffy. Beat in eggs and vanilla. Beat in flour mixture.

Divide dough in half. Roll one half dough between waxed paper to a 12x10-inch rectangle. Remove top sheet of waxed paper. Spread with half of filling. Roll up, beginning at the long side. Seal end and edge of dough. Wrap in waxed paper; chill well. Repeat procedure with remaining dough.

Preheat oven to 350°.
Cut dough into ¼-inch thick slices. Place 2 inches apart on greased baking sheets. Bake about 10 minutes. Cool on a wire rack.

Makes about 4 dozen.

RHUBARB SHORTBREAD

A nice treat for afternoon tea.

Filling
- 1 pound rhubarb, cut into 1-inch pieces
- ½ cup granulated sugar
- ½ cup water
- 1 teaspoon pure vanilla extract

Crust
- 4 cups all-purpose flour
- 2 teaspoons baking powder
- ¼ teaspoon salt
- 1 pound butter, room temperature
- 4 egg yolks
- 2 cups granulated sugar
- ½ teaspoon pure vanilla extract
- powdered sugar

Filling: Place rhubarb, sugar, water and vanilla into a saucepan. Simmer over low heat, stirring often, until rhubarb is soft, about 10 minutes. Remove from pan; place in a bowl, and cool.

Crust: Mix flour, baking powder and salt in a mixer bowl. Beat butter in another bowl on high speed, using the paddle attachment, until fluffy. Add egg yolks, granulated sugar and vanilla; beat until sugar is dissolved. Reduce speed to low; add flour mixture, and mix only until incorporated. Remove dough; cut into two pieces. Shape each into a ball. Wrap in food plastic wrap and freeze until firm.

Preheat oven to 350°.
Grate one ball of frozen dough with a box grater using the large holes, into an ungreased 13x9-inch baking dish. Pat gently to make an even layer, but do not press. Spread with the rhubarb filling. Grate the remaining frozen dough evenly over filling. Press lightly. Bake about 35–40 minutes. Remove from oven; immediately sprinkle with powdered sugar. Cool on a wire rack; cut into bars. Refrigerate leftovers.

If you don't want to grate the dough, crumble it gently and evenly into baking dish...but do not press the bottom layer.

Makes 2 dozen bars.

Pies

APPLE-RHUBARB PIE

Apple and rhubarb pie...serve with a scoop of vanilla ice cream.

9-inch double pie crust, unbaked

**1 12-ounce package frozen sliced apples, defrosted
   following package directions**
1½ cups granulated sugar
2 tablespoons quick-cooking tapioca
1 tablespoon finely grated fresh orange peel
⅛ teaspoon salt
2 eggs, slightly beaten
1 teaspoon pure vanilla extract
2 cups fresh rhubarb, sliced into 1-inch pieces

2 tablespoons milk
1 teaspoon granulated sugar

Preheat oven to 425°.
Line a 9-inch baking pie plate with one crust.

In a bowl, mix sugar, tapioca, orange peel, salt, eggs and vanilla extract.
Stir in apples and rhubarb. Spoon mixture into pie crust. Top with remaining
crust. Cut slits in top crust to let steam escape; brush lightly with milk and
sprinkle with 1 teaspoon granulated sugar. Bake 50 minutes or until crust
is golden brown. Cool slightly before serving. Refrigerate leftovers.

Makes 8 servings.

BERRY BERRY RHUBARB PIE

Raspberries and blueberries paired with rhubarb...a colorful pie.

9-inch double pie crust, unbaked

Filling
1¼ cups fresh raspberries
1¼ cups fresh blueberries
1¼ cups fresh rhubarb, chopped
1 tablespoon fresh lemon juice
1 teaspoon pure vanilla extract
1¼ cups granulated sugar
¼ cup quick-cooking tapioca
¼ teaspoon ground nutmeg
¼ teaspoon ground cinnamon
¼ teaspoon salt

Preheat oven to 400°.
Crust: Line a 9-inch baking pie plate with unbaked bottom crust; set aside.

Filling: Mix berries, rhubarb, lemon juice and vanilla in a large bowl; toss gently. In another bowl, mix sugar, tapioca, nutmeg, cinnamon and salt until blended. Carefully stir into fruit mixture. Spoon mixture into prepared crust. Cut remaining crust into ½-inch wide strips, and form a lattice crust for top of pie. Seal and flute edges. Bake 20 minutes. Reduce heat to 350° and continue baking 30 minutes or until filling is bubbly and crust golden brown. Cool. Refrigerate leftovers.

Makes 6 servings.

BLACKBERRY-RASPBERRY-RHUBARB PIE

Serve at room temperature with vanilla ice cream or whipped topping.

9-inch double pie crust, unbaked

Filling
1 cup fresh blackberries
1 cup fresh raspberries
2 cups fresh rhubarb,
  cut into ½-inch pieces
¾ cup granulated sugar
¼ cup all-purpose flour

1 tablespoon butter, melted
1 teaspoon fresh lemon juice
1 teaspoon pure vanilla extract

2 tablespoons light cream
2 tablespoons granulated
  sugar mixed with ⅛ teaspoon
  ground cinnamon

Filling: Mix berries and rhubarb in a glass bowl. In another bowl, mix sugar and flour; sprinkle over fruit, and stir gently. Cover and refrigerate 6 hours.

Preheat oven to 400°.
Line a 9-inch baking pie plate with unbaked bottom crust.

Stir melted butter, lemon juice and vanilla into fruit mixture. Spoon mixture into prepared unbaked crust. Cover with top crust. Crimp edges to seal. Cut several slits in top crust to let steam escape. Brush with light cream and sprinkle with sugar-cinnamon mixture. Bake 10 minutes.

Reduce heat to 350°; bake 45–50 minutes longer or until filling is bubbly and crust golden brown. Cool slightly before cutting. Refrigerate leftovers.

Makes 8 servings.

BLUEBERRY-RHUBARB PIE

Blueberries and rhubarb…a good pie.

9-inch double pie crust, unbaked

Filling
2 cups blueberries
1½ cups fresh rhubarb, cut into ½-inch pieces
1 cup granulated sugar
3 tablespoons all-purpose flour
⅛ teaspoon ground cinnamon
¾ teaspoon freshly grated lemon zest
1 teaspoon pure vanilla extract

Preheat oven to 400°.
Line a 9-inch baking pie plate with bottom crust, leaving a ½-inch overhang; set aside.

Filling: Place blueberries and rhubarb in a large bowl. In a small bowl, mix sugar, flour, cinnamon, lemon zest and vanilla; add to large bowl. Gently stir until well mixed. Pour mixture into prepared crust. Use the remaining crust to make a lattice top. Fold the overhang on the bottom crust back over the ends of lattice strips, and crimp for a decorative touch. Bake 15 minutes, then reduce heat to 350°. Bake 20–30 minutes or until filling is bubbly and crust is golden brown. Cool to room temperature before cutting. Refrigerate leftovers.

Makes 8 servings.

CHERRY-RHUBARB PIE

For extra color, add a few drops or red food coloring, if desired.

9-inch double pie crust, unbaked

Filling
4 cups fresh rhubarb, cut into ½-inch pieces
1 16-ounce can pitted tart cherries, drained
1½ cups granulated sugar
¼ cup quick-cooking tapioca
1 teaspoon pure vanilla extract
¼ teaspoon ground cinnamon, mixed
** with ⅛ teaspoon ground nutmeg**
1½ tablespoons cold butter, cut up

Preheat oven to 400°.
Line a 9-inch baking pie plate with bottom crust; set aside.

Filling: Mix rhubarb, cherries, sugar, tapioca and vanilla in a large bowl; let stand 15 minutes, then pour into prepared crust. Sprinkle with cinnamon mixture, and dot with butter.

Using remaining pie crust, form a lattice for top, by placing ½-inch wide strips of dough lengthwise spacing at 1-inch intervals. Fold back alternate strips; fold up as you weave crosswise strips over and under. Trim even along outer rim of pie; seal edges. Dampen edge of pie slightly with water, and place extra strips around entire rim of pie, covering ends of lattice. Flute edge while pressing to seal. Bake 40–50 minutes, or until filling is bubbly and crust golden brown. Refrigerate leftovers.

Makes 8 servings.

CLASSIC RHUBARB PIE

Using purchased pie crust dough makes pie-baking easy.

9-inch double pie crust, unbaked

Filling
4 cups fresh red rhubarb, cut into ½-inch pieces
1½ cups granulated sugar, or to taste
⅓ cup all-purpose flour
2 tablespoons butter, cut up

Glaze
1 tablespoon whole milk
1 teaspoon granulated sugar

Preheat oven to 400°.
Line a 9-inch baking pie plate with one crust, leaving an overhang; set aside.

Filling: Mix rhubarb and sugar in a large bowl. Stir in flour. Spoon mixture into the prepared unbaked pie crust. Dot with butter. Use remaining crust to weave a lattice top.

Glaze: Brush with milk, and sprinkle with sugar.

Cover edge with foil to prevent browning too fast. Bake 20 minutes. Reduce heat to 325°; remove foil; bake 30 minutes or until filling in center is bubbly and crust is browned. Cool to room temperature before serving. Refrigerate.

Makes 8 servings.

COCONUT-TOPPED RHUBARB-PEACH PIE

Fresh rhubarb and peaches with a coconut macaroon topping.

1 9-inch baked pie crust

Filling
1 egg, beaten
1 orange, juiced
½ teaspoon fresh grated orange peel
1 pound (2 to 2½ cups) fresh rhubarb, chopped
12 ounces (1½ to 2 cups) peaches, peeled and sliced
1 teaspoon pure vanilla extract

5 tablespoons all-purpose flour
¾ cup granulated sugar
¼ cup brown sugar, packed
¼ teaspoon ground nutmeg
½ teaspoon salt

Topping
2½ cups crumbled coconut macaroons
¾ cup whole pecans
¼ cup brown sugar, packed
6 tablespoons cold butter, cut up

Preheat oven to 375°.
Filling: Place first six filling ingredients in a large bowl. Mix the next five filling ingredients in another bowl until blended; sprinkle over first mixture and toss until coated. Pour mixture into baked pie crust.

Topping: Process all topping ingredients in a food processor to coarse crumbs. Sprinkle over filling. Bake about 1 hour or until filling is bubbly. Cool before serving. Refrigerate leftovers.

Makes 8 servings.

CREAM CHEESE RHUBARB PIE

Rhubarb topped with cream cheese...almost cheesecake!

**1 9-inch single pie crust,
    unbaked**

Filling
**¼ cup cornstarch
1 cup granulated sugar
⅛ teaspoon salt
½ cup water
3 cups fresh rhubarb,
    cut into ½-inch pieces**

Topping
**1 8-ounce package cream cheese,
    softened
½ cup granulated sugar
2 eggs
¼ cup sour cream
1 teaspoon pure vanilla extract
sweetened whipped cream
2 tablespoons sliced almonds,
    toasted**

Preheat oven to 425°.
Line a baking pie plate with crust; set aside.

Filling: Stir cornstarch, sugar and salt in a saucepan until well mixed. Stir in water until well blended. Add rhubarb. Cook over medium heat, stirring often, until mixture boils and thickens. Pour mixture into prepared crust. Bake 10 minutes. Reduce heat to 325°. Remove pie from oven and add topping.

Topping: Beat cream cheese and sugar in a bowl until smooth. Beat in eggs, sour cream and vanilla. Spoon mixture over baked rhubarb filling. Bake at 325° for 30–35 minutes or until topping is set. Remove from oven; cool on a wire rack to room temperature, then refrigerate and chill well before serving. Garnish with sweetened whipped cream and sprinkle with almonds when serving. Refrigerate leftovers.

Makes 8 servings.

CRUMB-TOP RHUBARB PIE

Pecans and rhubarb with a buttery crumb topping…good.

Crust
1 cup-all purpose flour
⅛ teaspoon salt
3 tablespoons cold butter
2 tablespoons solid shortening
3 tablespoons ice cold water,
 approximately

Topping
1 cup all-purpose flour
⅔ cup granulated sugar
½ cup cold butter

Filling
1¼ cups granulated sugar
⅓ cup all-purpose flour
½ teaspoon ground cinnamon
¼ teaspoon ground nutmeg
4 cups fresh rhubarb,
 cut into ½-inch pieces
1 teaspoon pure vanilla extract
⅓ cup pecans, chopped

Preheat oven to 400°.
Crust: Mix flour and salt in a bowl; cut in butter and shortening to form coarse crumbs. Stir in just enough water with a fork to moisten mixture. Gather into a ball; roll out on a lightly floured surface to a 12-inch circle. Press dough onto bottom and sides of a 9-inch baking pie plate. Trim crust and flute edge; set aside.

Filling: Mix all ingredients except rhubarb, vanilla and pecans in a large bowl until blended. Add rhubarb; toss to coat. Spoon mixture into prepared crust; drizzle top with vanilla and sprinkle with pecans.

Topping: Mix all ingredients in a bowl until crumbly; sprinkle over rhubarb. Cover edge of crust with aluminum foil. Bake 50 to 60 minutes or until filling is bubbly and crust browned. Remove foil during last 10 minutes of baking. Remove from oven; cool slightly before cutting. Refrigerate leftovers.

Makes 8 servings.

IMPOSSIBLE RHUBARB PIE

Streusel-topped rhubarb pie…impossible not to like.

Filling
1 16-ounce package frozen rhubarb, thawed and drained
¾ cup whole milk
2 eggs
1 cup granulated sugar
½ cup prepared baking mix
2 tablespoons butter, softened
1 teaspoon ground cinnamon
¼ teaspoon ground nutmeg
1 teaspoon pure vanilla extract

Topping
½ cup prepared baking mix
¼ cup brown sugar, packed
2 tablespoons cold butter
¼ cup chopped nuts

Preheat oven to 375°.
Grease a 9-inch baking plate. Spoon rhubarb evenly into plate. Beat
remaining filling ingredients in a blender until smooth, about 15 seconds on
high speed. Pour mixture over rhubarb.

Topping: Mix baking mix and brown sugar in a bowl; cut in butter until
crumbly. Stir in nuts. Sprinkle over rhubarb mixture. Bake 35 to 45 minutes
or until a knife inserted in center comes out clean. Cool. Serve with sweetened whipped cream. Refrigerate leftovers.

Makes 8 servings.

NO-BAKE RHUBARB CREAM PIE

Top with sweetened whipped cream when serving.

9-inch baked pie shell

2 cups fresh rhubarb, cut into 1-inch pieces
1 cup granulated sugar
2 tablespoons butter, melted
¼ cup cream
3 egg yolks
2 tablespoons cornstarch dissolved in 2 tablespoons water
1 teaspoon pure vanilla extract

Place rhubarb and sugar in a saucepan over medium heat; cook, stirring often until tender. Add remaining ingredients; cook and stir until thick. Pour mixture into baked pie shell. Chill. Refrigerate leftovers.

Makes 8 servings.

ORANGE-APRICOT-RHUBARB PIE

Substitute 1 teaspoon of pure vanilla extract for vanilla bean, if desired.

9-inch double pie crust, unbaked

Filling
1¾ cups granulated sugar
1 2-inch piece vanilla bean, cut up
½ fresh orange, including peel,
   cut into chunks
1 20-ounce bag frozen rhubarb
½ cup fresh cranberries, coarsely chopped
½ cup dried apricots, thinly sliced
¼ cup all-purpose flour
1 tablespoon granulated sugar mixed with
   ⅛ teaspoon ground cinnamon

Topping
1 cup dairy sour cream
   mixed with 2 tablespoons
   packed brown sugar and
   ⅛ teaspoon freshly grated
   orange peel

Preheat oven to 400°.
Crust: Line a 9-inch baking pie plate with bottom crust; set aside.
Cut second crust into ½-inch wide strips; set aside.

Filling: Process sugar and vanilla bean in food processor until finely
chopped. Add orange; process until finely chopped. Place mixture in a
large bowl. Add rhubarb, cranberries, apricots and flour; toss to coat.
Spoon mixture into prepared bottom crust. Form a lattice with pastry strips
on top of pie. Pinch edges to seal strips to crust edge. Fold overhang
under strip ends so that crust is flush with edge of pie plate; crimp edges.
Sprinkle with sugar-cinnamon mixture. Bake 45–55 minutes or until filling
is bubbly and crust golden brown. Cool to room temperature. Serve with
sour cream topping. Refrigerate leftovers.

Makes 8 servings.

ORANGE-RHUBARB PIE

Serve with whipped topping; garnish with freshly shredded orange peel.

9-inch double pie crust, unbaked

Filling
2 eggs
1¾ cups granulated sugar
¼ cup all-purpose flour
⅛ teaspoon ground nutmeg
¼ cup fresh orange juice
½ teaspoon pure vanilla extract
4 cups fresh rhubarb, cut into ½-inch pieces

Preheat oven to 425°.
Line a 9-inch baking pie plate with bottom crust; set aside.

Filling: Beat eggs in a large bowl. Stir in sugar, flour, nutmeg, orange juice and vanilla extract to blend well. Stir in rhubarb. Pour mixture into prepared crust. Cover with top crust. Cut several slits in top crust to allow steam to escape. Bake 50 minutes or until filling is bubbly and crust is browned. Cool before cutting. Refrigerate leftovers.

Makes 8 servings.

PINEAPPLE-RHUBARB PIE

Top with whipped topping when serving, if desired.

9-inch double pie crust, unbaked

Filling
1¼ cups granulated sugar
¼ cup all-purpose flour
¼ teaspoon salt
2 eggs, lightly beaten
1 20-ounce can crushed pineapple, drained
1 teaspoon pure vanilla extract
4 cups fresh rhubarb, cut into ½-inch pieces

Preheat oven to 375°.
Crust: Line a 9-inch baking pie plate with bottom crust; set aside.

Filling: Mix sugar, flour and salt in a large bowl until blended. Stir in eggs, pineapple, vanilla and rhubarb. Pour mixture into prepared crust. Cover with top crust. Cut several slits in top crust to allow steam to escape. Bake 35–45 minutes or until filling is bubbly and crust is golden brown. Cool before cutting. Refrigerate leftovers.

Makes 8 servings.

RHUBARB CREAM PIE

Rhubarb cream pie…a favorite.

9-inch single pie crust, unbaked

Filling
2 cups fresh rhubarb, finely diced
3 egg yolks, beaten
½ cup light cream (half & half)
1¼ cups granulated sugar
½ teaspoon salt
2 tablespoons all-purpose flour

Meringue
3 egg whites
6 tablespoons granulated sugar

Preheat oven to 400°.
Crust: Line a 9-inch baking pie plate with unbaked crust; set aside.

Filling: Spoon rhubarb into prepared crust. Mix eggs and cream in a large bowl. Stir in sugar, salt and flour. Pour mixture over rhubarb. Bake 10 minutes. Reduce heat to 350°, and continue baking an additional 45 minutes. Remove from oven.

Meringue: Beat egg whites with an electric beater to soft peaks. Beat in sugar, a little at a time, to form stiff peaks. Spread meringue over rhubarb to seal pie. Return to oven. Bake until light brown, about 8–10 minutes. Cool. Refrigerate.

Makes 8 servings.

RHUBARB CROUSTADE

Croustade...French for crust. This is the type of pastry my mother often used with different fillings. We just called it pie!

Crust
½ cup walnuts, toasted
1½ cups all-purpose flour
2 tablespoons powdered sugar
1 teaspoon finely grated fresh
    lemon zest
½ teaspoon salt
6 tablespoons cold butter, cut up
4 to 5 tablespoons ice water,
    approximately
2 tablespoons cornmeal

Filling
¾ pound rhubarb, cut into
    1-inch pieces
1 pint fresh strawberries,
    cleaned and halved
2 tablespoon cornstarch
1 tablespoon fresh lemon juice
1 teaspoon pure vanilla extract
½ cup granulated sugar, divided

Crust: Grind walnuts in a food processor using steel blade. Add flour, powdered sugar, lemon zest and salt; process until mixed. Add butter; process until mixture resembles coarse meal. Add 4 tablespoons water; process just until a ball forms, adding more water if necessary. Remove from processor; flatten dough into a dish. Wrap in food plastic wrap; chill 1 hour.

Preheat oven to 400°.
Lightly grease a baking sheet; sprinkle with cornmeal.

Filling: Mix all ingredients except 2 tablespoons granulated sugar in a bowl.

Roll out chilled dough on a lightly floured surface into a 14-inch round. Place on prepared baking sheet. Spoon filling mixture evenly over crust, leaving a 2-inch border all over. Sprinkle with 2 tablespoons granulated sugar. Fold the border over the filling. Bake 35–40 minutes, or until fruit is bubbly. Serve warm.

Makes 6 servings.

RHUBARB CUSTARD PIE

Rhubarb in a tasty custard filling.

9-inch double pie crust

Filling
1½ cups granulated sugar
¼ cup all-purpose flour
¼ teaspoon ground nutmeg
⅛ teaspoon salt

3 eggs, beaten
1 teaspoon pure vanilla extract
4 cups fresh rhubarb, cut into 1-inch pieces
2 tablespoons butter, cut up

Preheat oven to 400°.
Line a 9-inch baking pie plate with bottom crust; set aside.

Filling: Mix sugar, flour, nutmeg and salt in a large bowl. Stir in eggs, vanilla and rhubarb to coat well. Spoon mixture into prepared crust. Dot with butter. Cover with top crust; seal. Cut two slits on top crust to allow steam to escape. Bake 50 minutes. Cool. Store in refrigerator.

Makes 8 servings.

RHUBARB HUMBLE PIE

Nothing humble about the flavor…serve warm or chilled.

1 9-inch baked crust

Filling
2½ cups fresh rhubarb, sliced
2 cups water

2 eggs
1 cup evaporated milk
¾ cup granulated sugar
2 tablespoons all-purpose flour
2 tablespoons butter, melted and cooled
1½ teaspoons pure vanilla extract
½ teaspoon ground nutmeg

Preheat oven to 350°.
Filling: Bring rhubarb and water to a boil in a medium saucepan; let stand 2 minutes, then drain well. Spoon rhubarb into baked pie crust.

Beat remaining ingredients in a bowl; pour mixture over rhubarb. Cover with baking foil; bake 25 minutes. Remove foil, and continue baking until center is almost set, about 15–20 minutes. Refrigerate leftovers.

Makes 8 servings.

RHUBARB-LEMON CHIFFON PIE

Lemon and rhubarb…perfect for pie.

1 9-inch baked pastry shell

Filling
1 3-ounce package lemon-flavored gelatin
1 cup boiling water
½ cup granulated sugar
2 teaspoons finely shredded fresh lemon peel
3 tablespoons fresh lemon juice
1 cup whipping cream, whipped to soft peaks

Sauce
1½ cups granulated sugar
1 tablespoon water
1 tablespoon finely shredded fresh orange peel
6 cups fresh rhubarb, cut into ½-inch pieces
1 teaspoon pure vanilla extract

Filling: Stir gelatin, water and sugar in a bowl until dissolved. Add lemon peel and juice. Cover and chill until mixture mounds a little, but not set. Stir in whipped cream.

Sauce: In a saucepan, bring first three ingredients to a boil. Stir in rhubarb; simmer until tender, about 8 minutes, stirring often. Remove from heat; stir in vanilla. Refrigerate until cold, then stir into gelatin mixture. Chill until mixture mounds. Spoon into baked pastry shell. Cover and chill until firm, about 8 hours. Store in refrigerator.

Makes 10 servings.

RHUBARB MAGIC PIE

A pie that tastes like strawberry shortcake…serve with whipped topping.

1 cup sifted all-purpose flour
1 teaspoon baking powder
½ teaspoon salt
2 tablespoons butter
1 egg, beaten
2 tablespoons milk
3 cups fresh rhubarb, chopped
1 3-ounce package strawberry-flavored gelatin
1 teaspoon pure vanilla extract

½ cup all-purpose flour
1 cup granulated sugar
½ teaspoon ground cinnamon
¼ cup butter, melted

Preheat oven to 350°.
Sift together flour, baking powder and salt in a bowl. Cut in butter. Add egg and milk; mix. Press mixture into a greased 9-inch pie baking plate; top evenly with rhubarb. Sprinkle with gelatin; drizzle with vanilla.

In another bowl, mix flour, sugar, cinnamon and melted butter; sprinkle on top of pie. Bake 45–50 minutes or until rhubarb is tender. Cool before cutting. Refrigerate leftovers.

Makes 8 servings.

RHUBARB MERINGUE PIE

A pretty pie…tastes good too.

9-inch single pie crust, unbaked

Filling
2 eggs
1 cup granulated sugar
1 teaspoon pure vanilla extract
⅓ cup all-purpose flour
4 cups fresh rhubarb, cut into ½-inch pieces
2 tablespoons butter

Meringue
3 egg whites
¼ teaspoon cream of tartar
¼ cup granulated sugar

Preheat oven to 475°.
Crust: Press unbaked crust firmly onto bottom and side of a 9-inch baking pie plate. Trim overhang 1-inch from rim of plate; fold and roll pastry under even with plate; flute edges. Prick bottom and side of pastry thoroughly with fork. Bake 8 minutes or until light brown; cool on a rack.

Filling: Reduce heat to 375°. Beat eggs and sugar with an electric beater until thickened. Stir in vanilla, flour and rhubarb. Pour mixture into baked pie crust. Dot with butter. Cover edge of crust with a strip of cooking foil. Bake 35–45 minutes or until rhubarb is tender. Remove from oven to a rack; remove foil.

Meringue: Beat egg whites and cream of tartar on high speed until foamy. Beat in sugar, 1 tablespoon at a time, and continue beating until stiff and glossy. Spread meringue over rhubarb to edge of crust. Bake until light brown, about 8 minutes. Cool on a rack. Refrigerate leftovers.

Makes 8 servings.

RHUBARB-PEACH PIE

Frozen rhubarb may be used...bake a little longer, about 75 minutes.

9-inch double pie crust, unbaked

Filling
4 cups fresh red rhubarb, cut into ½-inch pieces
1 16-ounce can cling peach slices in heavy syrup,
  drained and halved
1 8-ounce can pineapple tidbits in juice, drained
1 teaspoon pure vanilla extract
1½ cups granulated sugar
⅓ cup all-purpose flour

Glaze
milk
granulated sugar

Preheat oven to 350°.
Line a 9-inch baking pie plate with bottom crust; set aside.

Filling: Place all filling ingredients in a large bowl; mix well. Spoon mixture into unbaked pie crust. Cover with top crust. Cut several slits in top crust to allow steam to escape.

Glaze: Brush top crust lightly with milk, and sprinkle lightly with granulated sugar. Bake 65–70 minutes or until filling is bubbly in center and crust is golden brown. Cool to room temperature before serving. Serve with sweetened whipped cream. Refrigerate leftovers.

Makes 8 servings.

RHUBARB-RASPBERRY PIE

Top with a dollop of sweetened whipped cream when serving.

9-inch double pie crust

Filling
1¾ cups granulated sugar
⅓ cup all-purpose flour
4 cups fresh rhubarb, chopped
1 medium size tart cooking apple, peeled and coarsely shredded
1 cup raspberries

Preheat oven to 375°.
Press bottom crust into a 9-inch pie baking plate; set aside.

Filling: In a large bowl, stir sugar and flour to blend. Add rhubarb, apple and raspberries; toss to coat. Spoon mixture into unbaked crust. Cover with top crust. Cut several slits in top crust to allow steam to escape. Seal and flute edge. Cover edge with baking foil. Bake 25 minutes. Remove foil, and continue baking 20–25 minutes or until top is golden and fruit is tender. Cool before serving. Refrigerate leftovers.

Makes 8 servings.

RHUBARB-STRAWBERRY LAYERED PIE

A special dessert.

1 10-inch baked pie crust

Rhubarb layer
2 tablespoons butter
2 cups fresh red rhubarb,
  cut into ½-inch pieces
1 cup granulated sugar
3 tablespoons cornstarch mixed
  with ¼ cup granulated sugar
⅛ teaspoon salt
2 egg yolks, slightly beaten
¼ cup whipping cream
1 teaspoon pure vanilla extract

Cream cheese layer
1 3-ounce package cream cheese,
  softened
2 tablespoons powdered sugar
4 ounces frozen non-dairy whipped
  topping, thawed

Strawberry layer
2 cups fresh strawberries
4 teaspoons cornstarch mixed with
  ¼ cup granulated sugar and
  ⅛ teaspoon ground cinnamon

Meringue
4 egg whites
½ teaspoon cream of tartar
½ cup granulated sugar

Rhubarb layer: Melt butter in a medium saucepan over low heat. Add rhubarb and sugar; cook, stirring often, until tender. In a bowl, mix cornstarch mixture and salt. Stir in egg yolks and whipping cream. Add to rhubarb mixture in saucepan; cook and stir until thick; stir in vanilla. Refrigerate until cold; spoon into cooled baked pie crust.

Cream cheese layer: Beat cream cheese and powdered sugar in a bowl until blended. Beat in whipped topping; spread over rhubarb layer.

Strawberry layer: Cook all strawberry layer ingredients in a saucepan, stirring until thickened. Chill. Spread over cream cheese layer.

Preheat oven to 350°.

Meringue: Beat egg whites and cream of tartar to soft peaks. Beat in sugar to stiff peaks; spread over strawberry layer and seal to edge of crust. Bake until browned, about 10 minutes. Cool before serving. Refrigerate leftovers.

Makes 8 servings.

SOUR CREAM RHUBARB PIE

To save time, use a purchased unbaked pie crust.

Crust
1¼ cups all-purpose flour
¼ teaspoon salt
⅓ cup solid cold shortening
3 to 4 tablespoons ice cold water,
approximately

Topping
¼ cup brown sugar, packed
¼ cup all-purpose flour
3 tablespoons butter, cut up

Filling
2 eggs, slightly beaten
1 cup dairy sour cream
1½ cups granulated sugar
2 tablespoons all-purpose flour
1 teaspoon pure vanilla extract
¼ teaspoon salt
3 cups fresh rhubarb, chopped

Preheat oven to 450°.
Crust: In a bowl, mix flour and salt; cut in shortening with a pastry blender or two knives until mixture resembles small peas. Sprinkle water, a tablespoon at a time, and mix with a fork to moisten. Form dough into a ball. Roll out on a floured surface into a 12-inch circle; wrap dough around rolling pin; unroll into a 9-inch baking pie plate. Trim to ½-inch beyond edge of plate; fold under; crimp edges high. Do not prick pastry.

Filling: Mix first six filling ingredients in a bowl. Stir in rhubarb. Pour mixture into prepared crust. Cover edge of pie with cooking foil. Bake 15 minutes. Reduce heat to 350° and continue baking 20 minutes. Remove foil and add topping.

Topping: Mix all topping ingredients in a small bowl; sprinkle over rhubarb filling. Continue baking 20–25 minutes or until filling is set. Cool slightly, then store in refrigerator.

Makes 8 servings.

STRAWBERRY-ALMOND RHUBARB PIE

Almond-topped—a special pie.

**9-inch double pie crust,
 unbaked**

Filling
⅔ cup granulated sugar
¼ cup cornstarch
½ teaspoon ground nutmeg
¼ teaspoon salt

½ cup almond cake and pastry filling*
1 tablespoon fresh lemon juice
½ teaspoon pure vanilla extract
**3 cups fresh rhubarb, cut
 into ½-inch pieces**
3 cups fresh strawberries, sliced
1 tablespoon butter, cut up

1 egg white, slightly beaten
2 tablespoons sliced almonds

Preheat oven to 375°.
Fit bottom crust into a 9-inch pie baking plate; set aside.

Filling: Mix first four ingredients in a large bowl. Stir in almond filling, lemon juice and vanilla. Add rhubarb and strawberries; toss to coat. Spoon mixture into prepared crust. Top evenly with butter. Cover with top crust. Cut several slits on top crust to allow steam to escape. Seal and crimp edges. Cover edge of pie with cooking foil. Bake 25 minutes; remove foil. Brush top with egg white, and sprinkle with almonds; continue baking about 10 minutes or until filling is bubbly and crust is golden brown. Cool before cutting. Refrigerate leftovers.

*Do not use almond paste…almond cake and pie filling, such as "Solo", can be found in baking section next to baking chocolate, etc.

Makes 8 servings.

STRAWBERRY-RHUBARB PIE

Strawberry and rhubarb pie...an all-time favorite.

9-inch double pie crust

Filling
¾ cup granulated sugar
¼ cup cornstarch
¾ teaspoon ground cinnamon
⅛ teaspoon ground cloves
⅛ teaspoon salt
1 pint fresh strawberries, halved
1 pound fresh rhubarb, cut into 1-inch pieces
1 teaspoon pure vanilla extract
1 tablespoon butter, cut up

Preheat oven to 375°.
Line bottom crust into a 9-inch baking pie plate; set aside.

Filling: Mix first five ingredients in a large bowl until blended. Add strawberries, rhubarb and vanilla; toss to coat. Spoon mixture into prepared crust; dot with butter. Cover with top crust. Cut several slits in top crust to allow steam to escape. Tuck edges over and flute. Bake about 45 minutes or until filling is bubbly and crust golden brown. Cool to room temperature before cutting. Serve with vanilla ice cream or whipped topping. Refrigerate leftovers.

Makes 8 servings.

ZUCCHINI-RHUBARB PIE

Another delicious way to use zucchini!

**9-inch double pie crust,
  unbaked**

Filling
**2 eggs, lightly beaten
1½ cups granulated sugar
¼ cup all-purpose flour
1 teaspoon freshly grated orange peel
¼ teaspoon ground cinnamon
⅛ teaspoon ground cloves, scant
¼ teaspoon salt
1 teaspoon pure vanilla extract
3 cups fresh zucchini, peeled and chopped
3 cups fresh rhubarb, sliced**

Topping
**2 teaspoons granulated sugar
mixed with a pinch of ground
cinnamon**

Preheat oven to 400°.
Crust: Line a 9-inch baking pie plate with bottom crust; set aside.

Filling: Beat eggs and sugar in a large bowl. Stir in flour, orange peel, cinnamon, cloves and salt. Stir in vanilla, zucchini and rhubarb. Pour mixture into prepared unbaked crust. Cover with top crust; cut several slits in top crust to allow steam to escape. Sprinkle with topping mixture. Bake for 15 minutes, then reduce oven temperature to 350°. Bake for an additional 40 minutes or until rhubarb is tender. Cool before cutting. Serve with vanilla ice cream. Refrigerate leftovers.

Makes 8 servings.

Desserts
Frozen Desserts

APPLE-RHUBARB BETTY

This recipe brings to mind the Apple Betty I prepared some years ago.....
adding rhubarb gives it a special zing! Serve warm with sweetened whipped
cream or vanilla ice cream.

⅔ cup granulated sugar
1 tablespoon cornstarch
1 20-ounce package frozen rhubarb
2¼ cups apple pie filling
½ teaspoon pure vanilla extract

1½ cups cubed white bread
¾ cup graham cracker crumbs
¼ cup light brown sugar, packed
½ teaspoon ground cinnamon
½ teaspoon apple pie spice
3 tablespoons butter, melted

Preheat oven to 375°.
Mix sugar and cornstarch in a saucepan. Add rhubarb. Cook, stirring constantly, until thickened and bubbly. Remove from heat. Stir in pie filling and
vanilla; set aside.

Mix bread, cracker crumbs, brown sugar, and spices in a bowl; stir in melted
butter. Spoon half the rhubarb mixture into a buttered 1½-quart baking
dish. Sprinkle with half of the bread mixture. Repeat layers. Cover and
bake 20 minutes. Uncover and bake 10 minutes. Refrigerate leftovers.

Makes 6 servings.

APRICOT-RHUBARB CHEESECAKE

Serve this cheesecake for a special event.

Crust
⅔ cup graham cracker crumbs
¼ cup granulated sugar
¼ cup butter, melted and cooled

Filling
1½ cups granulated sugar
3 8-ounce packages cream cheese, softened
2 eggs
1 teaspoon pure vanilla extract
¼ cup apricot preserves, melted, strained and cooled

Topping
1 cup dairy sour cream
2 tablespoons granulated sugar
3 tablespoons rhubarb preserves
   mixed in a small bowl with
3 tablespoons apricot preserves

Preheat oven to 325°.
Crust: Mix all crust ingredients in a bowl; press onto bottom only of a
9-inch springform baking pan.

Filling: In a bowl, beat sugar and cream cheese until smooth. Beat in eggs
and vanilla. Spoon 2 cups of mixture onto prepared crust. Stir apricot preserves into remainder of filling. Spoon over first layer. Bake 60–70 minutes
or until set. Run a knife around cake to loosen sides of pan. Cool completely in pan on a wire rack.

Topping: Stir sour cream and sugar in a bowl; spread over cooled cheesecake. Gently swirl preserve mixture on top of sour cream. Refrigerate at
least 3 hours before serving. Refrigerate leftovers.

Makes 12 servings.

CHERRY-RHUBARB DESSERT

Serve with sweetened whipped cream or vanilla ice cream.

Crust
1 cup quick-cooking oatmeal
1 cup brown sugar, packed
⅛ teaspoon salt
½ cup butter
1 cup all-purpose flour

Topping
5 cups fresh rhubarb, diced
1 cup water
1 cup granulated sugar mixed with 3 tablespoons cornstarch
1 teaspoon pure vanilla extract
¼ teaspoon almond flavoring
1 21-ounce can cherry pie filling

Preheat oven to 350°.
Crust: Mix all crust ingredients in a bowl; spread half the mixture into a 13x9-inch baking pan.

Topping: Spoon rhubarb evenly over crust. Stir water and sugar-cornstarch mixture in a saucepan until clear and thickened. Stir in flavorings and cherry pie filling. Spread over rhubarb. Sprinkle with remaining crumb mixture. Bake 45 minutes. Serve warm. Refrigerate leftovers.

Makes 12 servings.

COCONUT MERINGUE RHUBARB DESSERT

Coconut-topped meringue and rhubarb…yummy!

Crust
1 cup all-purpose flour
1 tablespoon granulated sugar
¼ teaspoon ground cinnamon
½ cup butter

Filling
3 egg yolks, slightly beaten
1 cup granulated sugar
2 tablespoons all-purpose flour
¼ teaspoon salt
½ cup light cream (half & half)
1 teaspoon pure vanilla extract
2½ cups fresh rhubarb, diced

Meringue
3 egg whites
⅓ cup granulated sugar
1 teaspoon pure vanilla extract
⅓ cup flaked coconut

Preheat oven to 350°.
Crust: Mix flour, sugar and cinnamon in a bowl; cut in butter. Press mixture into a 9x9-inch square baking pan. Bake 10 minutes.

Filling: Stir all filling ingredients except rhubarb in a large bowl until blended. Stir in rhubarb. Pour mixture over hot crust. Bake 45 minutes.

Meringue: Beat egg whites in bowl until foamy. Beat in sugar, 1 tablespoon at a time, and continue beating until stiff and glossy. Beat in vanilla extract. Spread meringue over rhubarb mixture. Sprinkle with coconut. Bake until light brown, about 10 minutes. Cool before cutting. Refrigerate leftovers.

Makes 9 servings.

COCONUT-RHUBARB BREAD PUDDING

Coconut and rhubarb in a good bread pudding…serve with a dollop of whipped cream sprinkled with a pinch of ground cinnamon.

1 cup granulated sugar
¾ cup water
2 tablespoons butter
3 cups fresh rhubarb, cut into ½-inch pieces
1 egg, beaten
1 teaspoon pure vanilla extract

4 cups soft bread cubes, lightly toasted
1 cup shredded coconut, divided

Preheat oven to 325°.
Mix sugar and water in a saucepan; bring to a boil. Remove from heat. Add butter and rhubarb. Cover and let stand 15 minutes. Drain, reserving liquid. Blend liquid with egg and vanilla.

Mix bread, rhubarb mixture, egg mixture and ¾ cup coconut. Pour into a buttered 1-quart baking casserole. Sprinkle with remaining coconut. Bake 45 minutes or until set. Serve warm or cool. Refrigerate leftovers.

Makes 6 servings.

DELIGHTFUL RHUBARB HASH

Serve this creamy hash in dessert glasses.

1 cup whipping cream
2 tablespoons powdered sugar
½ teaspoon pure vanilla extract
½ cup miniature marshmallows, more if desired
1½ cups rhubarb sauce, thickened
2 tablespoons almonds, toasted and chopped

Beat cream, powdered sugar and vanilla to stiff peaks in a bowl. Fold in marshmallows. Layer one-fourth of cream mixture in a 1-quart glass serving dish, then one-third of the rhubarb sauce, then one-fourth of the almonds. Repeat twice. Top with remaining cream and almonds. Serve chilled. Refrigerate leftovers.

Makes 4 servings.

115

FIG AND RHUBARB COMPOTE

A colorful compote.

4½ cups water
3 cups granulated sugar
6 cups fresh rhubarb, cut into 1-inch pieces
2 fresh oranges, peel and white pith removed,
   cut into ½-inch slices, then halved
12 fresh figs, cut into quarters
2 tablespoons fresh orange zest
½ teaspoon pure vanilla extract

Place water and sugar in a 4-quart nonreactive pan; stir until dissolved.
Add rhubarb; bring to a boil. Reduce heat; cook, stirring occasionally, until
tender, but not falling apart. Remove rhubarb with a slotted spoon to a
large bowl; reserve liquid. Add orange slices and fig to bowl.

Add orange zest to liquid in pan; cook over medium-high heat 20 minutes;
stir in vanilla extract. Strain liquid and pour over the rhubarb, oranges and
figs in bowl. Chill well before serving. Refrigerate leftovers.

Makes 7 cups.

MARGARET'S RHUBARB DESSERT

A special dessert.

Crust
1 cup butter
2 cups all-purpose flour
2 tablespoons powdered sugar

Filling
6 egg yolks
2 cups granulated sugar
1 cup cream
1 teaspoon pure vanilla extract
4 tablespoons all-purpose flour
5 cups fresh rhubarb, sliced thin

Meringue
6 egg whites
¼ teaspoon salt
1 teaspoon pure vanilla extract
¾ cup granulated sugar

Preheat oven to 350°.
Crust: Mix butter, flour and powdered sugar in a bowl until well blended.
Pat into a 13x9-inch baking pan. Bake 10 minutes; remove from oven.

Filling: In a bowl, beat egg yolks and sugar. Stir in cream, vanilla and flour;
beat until smooth. Stir in rhubarb. Pour mixture over hot crust. Continue
baking 50–55 minutes.

Meringue: Beat egg whites to soft peaks. Add salt and vanilla, then continue beating to stiff peaks, gradually adding granulated sugar. Spread over
hot filling, increase heat to 400°. Bake until brown, about 8 minutes. Serve
warm or cold. Refrigerate leftovers.

Makes 12 servings.

PEAR AND RHUBARB COMPOTE

An elegant dessert.

½ cup dry red wine
¾ cup granulated sugar
½ teaspoon ground allspice
4 Bartlett pears, peeled, cored and cut into 1-inch pieces
1 20-ounce bag rhubarb, cut into 1-inch pieces
½ teaspoon pure vanilla extract

Bring wine, sugar and allspice to a simmer in a heavy saucepan over medium-low heat. Stir in pears, rhubarb and vanilla extract. Cover and simmer, stirring occasionally, until rhubarb and pears are just tender, about 8 minutes. Serve warm in dessert bowls topped with vanilla ice cream.

Makes 4 servings.

PINEAPPLE-RHUBARB ICE BOX CAKE

A nice dessert for warm summer days.

1½ cups gingersnap cookies (about 40), coarsely crushed
¼ cup butter, softened

1 8-ounce can pineapple chunks in juice, drained, reserve 3 tablespoons juice; cut chunks in half
¼ cup butter
1½ cups powdered sugar
1 8-ounce package cream cheese, softened
1 teaspoon pure vanilla extract

4 cups fresh rhubarb, cut into 1-inch pieces
½ cup granulated sugar
1 tablespoon cornstarch, mixed with ¼ cup water

12 whole gingersnaps
½ cup chopped nuts

Preheat oven to 350°.
Mix cookie crumbs and butter in a bowl; press onto bottom of an ungreased 8-inch square baking pan. Bake 5 minutes; cool.

In a bowl, beat 3 tablespoons pineapple juice, butter, powdered sugar, cream cheese and vanilla extract until smooth. Spread half the mixture over cooled crumbs.

Mix rhubarb and sugar in a saucepan. Add cornstarch mixture; bring to a boil, stirring constantly. Reduce heat to low; cover and simmer until rhubarb is tender, about 8 minutes. Cool, then refrigerate to chill. Spread over last layer. Then top with drained pineapple pieces.

Spread remaining cream cheese mixture over pineapple. Press whole ginger snaps lightly into top; sprinkle nuts around cookies. Cover and refrigerate until well chilled. Store in refrigerator.

Makes 12 servings.

QUICK RHUBARB COMPOTE

A good topping for ice cream, and thinly sliced pound cake.

5 cups fresh rhubarb, cut into 2-inch pieces
⅓ cup granulated sugar, or to taste
½ teaspoon freshly grated orange or lemon zest
¼ cup water
¼ cup currants
1 apple; peeled, cored and sliced
½ teaspoon pure vanilla extract

Bring all ingredients except vanilla to a boil in a saucepan. Reduce heat, cover and simmer, stirring often, until rhubarb is soft, about 10 minutes; stir in vanilla extract. Taste, and stir in more sugar if needed.

Makes 4 cups.

QUICK RHUBARB PUDDING

Serve this quick dessert warm or cold...thanks Sharon.

3 cups fresh rhubarb, sliced
1 cup water
½ cup granulated sugar
1 3½-ounce package cook-and-serve vanilla pudding mix

Mix rhubarb, water and sugar in a 2-quart glass microwave-safe bowl. Microwave uncovered 8 minutes or until rhubarb is softened. Stir in vanilla pudding; microwave until it boils, about 45 seconds to 1 minute.

Makes 4 servings.

RASPBERRY-RHUBARB BAKE

Baked raspberries and rhubarb...sweet and tangy. Serve this dessert with cinnamon vanilla ice cream or sweetened whipped cream.

1½ cups raspberries
¾ cup light brown sugar, packed
¼ cup boiling water

2 tablespoons butter, cut up
½ teaspoon pure vanilla extract
4 cups rhubarb, cut into ½-inch pieces

Preheat oven to 350°.
Place raspberries, sugar and water into a blender; process to puree, then strain through a sieve into a bowl.

Stir in remaining ingredients. Pour into a buttered 11x7-inch baking dish. Bake 15 minutes; stir and bake 15 minutes more or until rhubarb is soft. Remove from oven; cool slightly, then serve. Refrigerate leftovers.

Makes 4 servings.

RICE PUDDING WITH RHUBARB SAUCE

Top with a dollop of whipped cream for an extra taste treat.

Pudding
2 cups cooked long-grain rice
¼ cup granulated sugar
½ cup tub-style cream cheese
¼ cup milk
¼ cup evaporated milk
½ teaspoon pure vanilla extract
½ teaspoon ground cinnamon
⅛ teaspoon salt
1 large egg

Sauce
½ cup fresh rhubarb, thinly sliced
2 tablespoons apple cider
1 tablespoon granulated sugar
¼ teaspoon ground cinnamon

Preheat oven to 350°.
Pudding: Butter four 4-ounce baking casseroles. Spoon ½ cup rice into each. Beat sugar with cream cheese, until smooth, in a bowl. Add milks, vanilla, cinnamon, salt and egg; beat well. Spoon equal amount of mixture, over rice, into each casserole. Place casseroles in a 13x9-inch baking pan filled with hot water to a depth of 1 inch. Bake until set, about 40 minutes. Remove from water bath.

Sauce: Bring all sauce ingredients to a boil in a small saucepan. Reduce heat; cover and simmer 8 minutes, stirring often. Drizzle 1 tablespoon sauce over each serving rice pudding. Refrigerate leftovers.

Makes 4 servings.

RHUBARB BREAD PUDDING

Serve warm with cinnamon-topped sweetened whipped cream.

1 pound red rhubarb, cut into ½-inch pieces
¾ cup granulated sugar
12 slices white bread, crusts removed, buttered, using ¼ cup butter

Custard
2 cups whipping cream
1 cup whole milk
4 large eggs, lightly beaten
1 teaspoon pure vanilla extract
¾ cup granulated sugar

Topping
1 tablespoon granulated sugar
mixed with ⅛ teaspoon
ground cinnamon

Mix rhubarb and sugar in a glass bowl; let stand at room temperature one hour. Place 4 buttered bread slices, buttered side down, in a buttered 13x9-inch baking dish. Sprinkle with half the rhubarb mixture. Repeat layering once. Top with remaining buttered bread, buttered side down.

Custard: Mix all custard ingredients in a bowl to blend; pour over bread.

Topping: Sprinkle with sugar-cinnamon mixture. Cover and refrigerate at least two hours.

Preheat oven to 350°.
Place baking dish in a larger baking pan filled with water halfway up. Bake 1 hour or until top is golden and crisp. Serve warm. Refrigerate leftovers.

Makes 6 servings.

RHUBARB COMPOTE AND SORBET

A refreshing dessert.

7 cups fresh rhubarb, cut into 1-inch pieces
½ cup currant jelly
½ cup granulated sugar
¼ cup minced fresh apple
2 tablespoons fresh lemon juice
1 teaspoon freshly grated lemon peel
1 teaspoon pure vanilla extract
1 pint coconut sorbet

Bring all ingredients except vanilla extract and coconut sorbet to a boil in a nonreactive saucepan. Reduce heat; cover and simmer until slightly thickened, about 10 minutes. Stir in vanilla extract. Pour mixture into a glass serving bowl. Chill well before serving. Serve compote in dessert bowls topped with coconut sorbet. Freeze or refrigerate leftovers.

Makes 8 servings.

RHUBARB GINGER FOOL

This dessert is creamy and delicious…no fooling!

2 pounds fresh rhubarb, cut into 1-inch pieces
1¼ cups granulated sugar
2 tablespoons chopped candied ginger
2 tablespoons freshly grated ginger
1 teaspoon water

2 cups whipping cream
2 tablespoons powdered sugar
1 teaspoon pure vanilla extract

Place rhubarb, granulated sugar, gingers and water in a stainless-steel saucepan. Cover with a tight-fitting lid. Cook over low heat, stirring occasionally, until rhubarb is very tender, about 20 minutes. Spoon into a dish and chill well.

Whip cream with powdered sugar and vanilla to soft peaks; fold into chilled rhubarb mixture. Spoon into dessert glasses. Refrigerate leftovers.

Makes 6 servings.

RHUBARB GINGERSNAP PARFAIT

A tasty parfait.

4 cups fresh rhubarb, cut into 1-inch pieces
½ cup granulated sugar

¾ cups whipping cream
3 tablespoons powdered sugar
⅓ cup dairy sour cream
1 teaspoon pure vanilla extract
6 tablespoons finely ground gingersnaps (about 8)

Bring rhubarb and granulated sugar to a boil in a nonreactive heavy saucepan, stirring constantly. Reduce heat; simmer, stirring often, until rhubarb is very tender, about 20 minutes. Pour into a glass bowl; chill.

Beat whipping cream with powdered sugar to stiff peaks. Add sour cream and vanilla; beat again to stiff peaks. Layer ⅓ cup rhubarb, ½ cup whipped cream mixture and 1½ tablespoons gingersnap crumbs in 6-ounce parfait glasses. Serve chilled. Refrigerate leftovers.

Makes 4 servings.

RHUBARB SHORTCAKE

Rhubarb shortcake...another summertime treat.

Sauce
6 cups fresh red rhubarb,
   cut into 1-inch slices
¾ cup granulated sugar
¼ cup water
1 teaspoon pure vanilla extract

Shortcake
2 cups all-purpose flour
4 teaspoons baking powder
1 tablespoon granulated sugar
¼ teaspoon salt
¼ cup cold butter, cut into pieces
¾ cup whole milk
1 teaspoon sugar

sweetened whipped cream

Sauce: Bring rhubarb, sugar and water to a boil in a heavy nonreactive saucepan over high heat. Reduce heat to low and simmer, stirring often, until just tender and sauce is slightly thickened. Remove from heat; stir in vanilla. Cool in pan to room temperature.

Shortcake: Preheat oven to 400°. Mix flour, baking powder, sugar and salt in a large bowl. Cut in butter with pastry blender until mixture resembles coarse meal. Stir in milk with a fork. Knead just until a dough forms, about 2 minutes. Pat dough into a ¾-inch thick, 6-inch round. Cut into three 3-inch rounds with a biscuit cutter. Gather scraps of dough and form another biscuit. Place biscuits on an ungreased, heavy-duty baking sheet; space apart. Sprinkle with sugar. Bake 20 minutes. Split each biscuit in half horizontally while warm.

To serve, place bottom half of biscuit on a dessert plate. Top with rhubarb mixture. Place other half of biscuit on top. Top with sweetened whipped cream. Refrigerate leftovers.

Makes 4 servings.

RHUBARB SPRINKLE DESSERT

Pretty simple...this sprinkle.

4 cups fresh rhubarb, coarsely chopped
1 3-ounce package strawberry-flavored gelatin dessert mix
1 cup granulated sugar
1 cup water
1 package (18.25-ounce) yellow cake mix
½ cup coconut
½ cup nuts
¾ cup melted butter, do not substitute

Preheat oven to 325°.
Sprinkle ingredients in a greased 13x9-inch baking pan in order listed. DO NOT MIX. Bake until rhubarb is tender 25–35 minutes. Serve warm. Refrigerate leftovers.

Makes 12 servings.

SAUCY BLUEBERRY-RHUBARB DESSERT

This easy dessert is equally good served chilled or warm, topped with sweetened whipped cream.

1 pound fresh rhubarb, cut into 1-inch pieces
5 tablespoons granulated sugar
¼ cup fresh orange juice
½ teaspoon finely grated fresh orange zest
1 cup blueberries
1 teaspoon pure vanilla extract
2 navel oranges, peeled and cut into sections

Mix rhubarb, sugar, orange juice and orange zest in a saucepan. Bring to a boil; reduce heat and simmer, stirring often, until rhubarb is tender, about 8 minutes. Stir in blueberries and vanilla extract. Spoon mixture into dessert bowls; top each with orange sections. Refrigerate leftovers.

Makes 4 servings.

SCANDINAVIAN RHUBARB PUDDING

This dessert suits my Scandinavian husband…and I love it too.

1½ pounds fresh rhubarb, cut into ½-inch slices
1½ cups water
½ cup granulated sugar
½ teaspoon pure vanilla extract
3 tablespoons cornstarch, dissolved in 2 tablespoons water
1 cup heavy cream
¼ cup granulated sugar
1 teaspoon pure vanilla extract

Simmer rhubarb, water and ½ cup sugar in a saucepan, stirring often, until soft. Stir in ½ teaspoon vanilla. Stir in cornstarch mixture; cook, stirring constantly, until thickened and clear. Pour mixture into a glass serving dish. Chill well.

Whip cream in a bowl until frothy. Add ¼ cup sugar and 1 teaspoon vanilla extract; whip until stiff.

Spoon chilled pudding into dessert glasses; top with whipped cream. Refrigerate leftovers.

Makes 4 servings.

SPONGE PUDDING WITH RHUBARB

Rhubarb sauce over pudding…a real treat.

Pudding
2 tablespoons butter, softened
½ cup plus 1 tablespoon granulated sugar
⅛ teaspoon salt
2 teaspoons freshly grated lemon zest
2 large egg yolks
3 tablespoons all-purpose flour
3 tablespoons fresh lemon juice
1 tablespoon orange juice
¾ cup whole milk
3 large egg whites

Sauce
1½ cups fresh rhubarb, cut into ½-inch dice
3 tablespoons granulated sugar
1 tablespoon water
½ teaspoon pure vanilla extract

Preheat oven to 325°.
Pudding: Place 2 tablespoons butter, sugar and salt in mixer bowl. Using paddle attachment, mix on medium speed until crumbly. Mix in lemon zest and egg yolks; then mix in flour, lemon juice, orange juice and milk. Beat egg whites in a separate bowl until stiff. Whisk in egg yolk mixture. Butter four 6-ounce custard cups; coat with sugar. Spoon pudding into each cup. Line a baking pan with a tea towel; place cups on towel. Fill pan halfway with hot water. Bake until set, about 25 minutes. Cool custard cups on wire rack. Refrigerate to chill.

Sauce: Cook rhubarb with sugar and water, stirring often, until tender, about 6 minutes. Stir in vanilla. Cool.

To serve, invert puddings on dessert plates. Spoon rhubarb sauce on top. Refrigerate leftovers.

Makes 4 servings.

STRAWBERRY-RHUBARB CHEESECAKE

When serving, top with a dollop of sweetened whipped cream.

Crust
¾ cup margarine, softened
⅓ cup brown sugar, packed
1½ cups all-purpose flour
½ cup pecans, chopped

Filling
2 8-ounce packages cream
   cheese, softened
2 eggs
¾ cup granulated sugar
1½ teaspoons pure vanilla extract

Topping
3 cups rhubarb, chopped
1 cup fresh strawberries, sliced
1 cup granulated sugar
¼ cup water
4 teaspoons cornstarch

Preheat oven to 375°.
Crust: Lightly grease a 13x9-inch baking pan. Mix all crust ingredients in a bowl. Press onto bottom of prepared pan. Bake 10 minutes.

Filling: Beat all filling ingredients in a bowl; pour over baked crust. Return to oven and bake 20–25 minutes or until set. Cool slightly.

Topping: Mix rhubarb, strawberries and sugar in a large saucepan. Cook until bubbly over medium heat, stirring often. In a small bowl, mix water and cornstarch until dissolved; stir into rhubarb mixture; cook and stir until thickened. Cool, then spread over cheesecake. Chill 8 hours. Store in refrigerator.

Makes 12 servings.

STRAWBERRY-RHUBARB COMPOTE

Yummy over cake.

4 cups rhubarb, cut into ½-inch pieces
½ cup granulated sugar
2 tablespoons water
1 16-ounce package frozen sliced sweetened strawberries, thawed
½ teaspoon pure vanilla extract
¼ teaspoon ground cinnamon
¼ teaspoon ground nutmeg

Bring rhubarb, sugar and water to a boil in a heavy saucepan. Reduce heat; cover and cook, stirring occasionally, just until tender, about 5 minutes. Remove from heat. Stir in remaining ingredients. Chill well before serving. Refrigerate leftovers.

Makes about 3½ cups.

STRAWBERRY-RHUBARB DESSERT

A tasty dessert made easy with purchased crescent dinner rolls.

2 cups fresh rhubarb, cut into 1-inch pieces
1 cup granulated sugar
¼ cup fresh orange juice
1 teaspoon pure vanilla extract
2 cups sliced frozen unsweetened strawberries, thawed

1 8-ounce can refrigerated crescent dinner rolls
1 tablespoon granulated sugar mixed with
  1 teaspoon freshly grated orange peel
1 teaspoon granulated sugar

sweetened whipped cream

Preheat oven to 375°.
Mix rhubarb, sugar and orange juice in a nonreactive saucepan. Cook over medium heat, stirring often, until rhubarb is tender, about 15 minutes. Remove from heat; cool 15 minutes. Stir in vanilla extract and strawberries.

Unroll dough; press perforation lines until sealed. Sprinkle with sugar and orange peel mixture. Starting at the short side, roll up dough; seal edges. Cut roll crosswise into 6 equal slices; place cut side down on a greased baking sheet. Sprinkle with 1 teaspoon sugar. Bake about 14–16 minutes. Cool 10 minutes; place in individual dessert bowls. Top each with rhubarb mixture and plenty of whipped cream. Refrigerate leftovers

Makes 6 servings.

STRAWBERRY-RHUBARB TIRAMISU

Serve on dessert plates…garnish each portion with a whole strawberry.

4 cups fresh rhubarb, sliced
¾ cup granulated sugar
1 teaspoon pure vanilla extract
1 pint strawberries, sliced

1½ (3-ounce each) packages
    ladyfingers

3 large egg yolks
⅓ cup granulated sugar
1 teaspoon pure vanilla extract
¼ cup water
1 cup mascarpone cheese (8-ounces)
1½ cups heavy cream, whipped to stiff peaks

Place rhubarb and sugar in a medium saucepan; bring to a boil, stirring constantly. Reduce heat; cook, stirring often, 15 minutes or until rhubarb is soft; stir in vanilla and strawberries. Pour into a bowl, and refrigerate, stirring occasionally, until cold.

Place egg yolks, sugar, pure vanilla and water into the top of a double boiler. Cook mixture over boiling water, stirring constantly, until mixture thickens, about 10 minutes. Pour into a bowl, and whisk until cool. Whisk in mascarpone cheese until blended. Fold in whipped cream.

Place half of the ladyfingers onto bottom of a 2-quart glass serving dish. Spread with half the rhubarb mixture. Cover with half the cheese-cream mixture. Repeat layering, ending with cheese-cream mixture. Chill before serving. Refrigerate leftovers.

Makes 16 servings.

STRAWBERRY-RHUBARB TRIFLE

Garnish with fresh strawberries when serving.

2 cups fresh rhubarb, cut into ½-inch pieces
1 cup granulated sugar
¼ cup fresh orange juice
1 teaspoon pure vanilla extract
2 cups strawberries, sliced

2 packages (4-serving size) cook and serve vanilla pudding mix
2½ cups whole milk
2 cups frozen nondairy whipped topping, thawed

1 16-ounce pound cake
½ cup orange marmalade

Bring rhubarb, sugar and orange juice to a boil in a 2-quart saucepan over medium heat. Reduce heat to low; cook, stirring occasionally, until rhubarb is tender and thickened slightly; stir in vanilla extract. Remove from heat; cool 30 minutes. Refrigerate until chilled. Stir in strawberries.

Cook pudding and milk in a 2-quart saucepan over medium heat, stirring constantly, until mixture boils. Cool in pan 15 minutes, then refrigerate and chill well. Fold in whipped topping.

Cut pound cake horizontally in half. Spread marmalade over bottom half. Top with top half. Cut into 18 slices. Place 9 slices in bottom of a 3–quart trifle or glass serving bowl. Spoon half the rhubarb mixture over cake; top with half the pudding. Repeat layers with remaining cake, rhubarb and pudding. Cover and refrigerate until chilled. Refrigerate leftovers.

Makes 12 servings.

FROZEN RHUBARB CUSTARD

Gather the family for this tempting frozen custard.

2 cups fresh rhubarb, cut into 1-inch pieces
¼ cup water

2 cups half & half (light cream)
3 eggs beaten
1¼ cups granulated sugar
1 cup whipping cream
1 teaspoon freshly grated orange peel
1 teaspoon pure vanilla extract
3 drops red food coloring, optional

Cover and simmer rhubarb and water in a medium saucepan until tender, about 10 minutes. Puree in food processor or blender.

Mix half & half, eggs and sugar in a medium saucepan. Cook, stirring constantly, over low heat until mixture thickens and coats a metal spoon. Stir in pureed rhubarb, whipping cream, orange peel, vanilla and food coloring. Pour mixture into ice cream machine canister. Freeze in an ice cream maker following manufacturer's directions.

Makes 6 servings.

FROZEN RHUBARB YOGURT

Rhubarb frozen yogurt…refreshing treat.

2 cups rhubarb, chopped

½ cup plain low fat yogurt
3 tablespoons granulated sugar
2 tablespoons fresh orange juice

Cook rhubarb with a little water in a saucepan until tender; cool.

Puree cooked rhubarb in a food processor until smooth. Stir in remaining ingredients until well blended. Freeze in ice cream maker following manufacturer's directions.

Or, place mixture in a shallow metal pan; cover and freeze until almost firm, about 3–4 hours. Break up mixture and process in food processor, in batches if necessary, until smooth, then freeze in an airtight container 1 hour or until firm.

Makes 4 servings.

RHUBARB ICE

Serve in sherbet glasses, and garnish with fresh strawberries.

4 cups rhubarb, cut into small pieces
1½ cups granulated sugar
¼ teaspoon salt
1 cup water
chopped rind of 1 fresh lemon

4 tablespoons fresh lemon juice

Cook all ingredients except lemon juice in a saucepan, stirring often, until rhubarb is tender; press mixture through a sieve. Stir in lemon juice. Freeze in any nonreactive, freezer-safe container until firm. When serving, scrape up thin layers of the ice with an inverted spoon, and beat back and forth in container until texture is smooth. Serve immediately.

Makes 6 servings.

RHUBARB ICE CREAM

Rhubarb ice cream for dessert...look for company.

Rhubarb sauce
1½ cups granulated sugar
1 tablespoon water
1 tablespoon finely shredded fresh orange peel
6 cups fresh rhubarb, cut into ½-inch pieces

6 cups heavy whipping cream
1 cup granulated sugar
2 teaspoons pure vanilla extract
3 cups rhubarb sauce, listed above

Rhubarb sauce: Mix sugar, water and orange peel in a saucepan to blend; bring to a boil. Stir in rhubarb. Reduce heat; simmer uncovered, stirring often, until rhubarb is tender and mixture is thickened. Cool, then refrigerate.

Heat whipping cream in a saucepan over medium heat until bubbles begin to appear around edge of pan. Slowly add sugar; cook, stirring constantly, 2–3 minutes or until sugar is dissolved. Immediately place saucepan in another pan of ice water. Cool to room temperature. Stir in vanilla. Pour mixture into a large bowl. Cover and chill in refrigerator at least 4 hours. Stir in 3 cups rhubarb sauce. Pour mixture into a 1-gallon ice cream freezer. Freeze according to manufacturer's directions.

Makes 3 quarts.

RHUBARB-RASPBERRY ICE CREAM

When serving, spoon a little of the reserved sauce over top.

Puree
5 cups fresh rhubarb, cut into ½-inch pieces
1 cup granulated sugar
2 tablespoons light corn syrup
⅛ teaspoon salt
½ teaspoon pure vanilla extract
1 cup frozen unsweetened raspberries, thawed, include juice

Custard
6 large egg yolks
½ cup heavy whipping cream
½ cup granulated sugar
2 tablespoons light corn syrup
1 teaspoon pure vanilla extract

Puree: Cook rhubarb, sugar, corn syrup and salt in a heavy saucepan over medium-low heat, stirring often, until rhubarb is tender, about 10 minutes. Puree mixture in a blender. Add vanilla and thawed raspberries including juice; puree until smooth.

Custard: Whisk egg yolks, whipping cream, sugar, corn syrup and vanilla in a heavy saucepan until blended. Cook, stirring constantly, over medium-low heat, until it is thickened and coats a metal spoon, about 7 minutes, do not boil. Remove from heat. Stir in 2½ cups rhubarb puree. Refrigerate until cold. (Reserve remaining puree for topping). Freeze custard in an ice cream maker according to manufacturer's directions. Store frozen ice cream in a covered container.

Makes about 4 cups.

RHUBARB SHERBET

A refreshing dessert.

2½ cups fresh rhubarb, cut into ½-inch pieces
2 8-ounce cans crushed pineapple
½ cup granulated sugar
⅛ teaspoon salt
1⅔ cups evaporated milk, chilled
⅛ teaspoon mace or nutmeg

Simmer rhubarb, pineapple, sugar and salt in a saucepan, stirring often, until rhubarb is tender. Remove from heat. Press through a coarse sieve. There should be 2 cups pulp and syrup. Chill. Whip milk until very stiff; fold into rhubarb mixture. Stir in mace or nutmeg and pour into any nonreactive, freezer-safe container. Freeze until firm.

Makes 10 servings.

RHUBARB SLUSH

A refreshing slush.

3 cups rhubarb, cut into 1-inch pieces
1 cup water
⅓ cup granulated sugar
1 cup apple juice
1 6-ounce container frozen pink lemonade concentrate, thawed

1 bottle lemon-lime carbonated beverage

Bring rhubarb, water and sugar to a boil in a large saucepan. Reduce heat; cover and simmer until rhubarb is tender, about 8 minutes. Cool slightly.

Process half of the mixture into a food processor until smooth. Pour into a medium bowl. Repeat with remaining rhubarb mixture. Stir in apple juice and lemonade concentrate. Pour mixture into an 8x8x2-inch baking pan. Cover and freeze until firm about 3 hours.

To serve, let stand at room temperature 45 minutes. Spoon ⅓ cup mixture into each glass; fill with ⅓ cup carbonated beverage. Freeze leftovers.

Makes 12 servings.

RHUBARB SORBET

A cool treat.

1 cup plus 2 tablespoons granulated sugar
1 cup water
1 pound fresh rhubarb, cut into 1-inch pieces
2 tablespoons light corn syrup
½ teaspoon pure vanilla extract

Stir sugar and water in a saucepan over low heat until sugar dissolves. Bring to a boil; add rhubarb, then reduce heat and simmer, stirring often, until rhubarb is tender, about 10 minutes. Puree mixture in food processor until smooth. Stir in corn syrup and vanilla. Chill 1 hour. Pour mixture in an ice cream maker and freeze according to manufacturer's directions.

Makes about 4 cups.

Tarts
Tortes

ALMOND RHUBARB TART

Almonds and rhubarb in a butter pastry.

Crust
1¼ cups all-purpose flour
¼ cup granulated sugar
½ cup butter, cut up
1 egg yolk

Filling
4 cups fresh rhubarb, cut into
  1-inch pieces
¼ cup water
1 cup granulated sugar, divided
1 cup blanched almonds
6 tablespoons butter, cut up
2 eggs
½ teaspoon vanilla extract
⅛ teaspoon almond extract

Preheat oven to 300°.
Crust: Mix flour and sugar in a bowl; cut in butter until fine crumbs form.
Stir in egg yolk with a fork until dough holds together; form into a ball.
Press dough onto bottom and up sides of a 10-inch tart pan with remov-
able bottom. Bake until slightly brown, about 18 minutes.

Filling: Bring rhubarb, water and 5 tablespoons granulated sugar to a boil in
a saucepan over medium-low heat; cook and stir 2 minutes. Remove from
heat; drain; set aside. Process almonds in food processor to a powder. Add
remaining sugar, butter, eggs and extracts. Process until blended. Pour mixture into prepared crust. Top with drained rhubarb. Increase oven to 350°.
Bake 40–50 minutes. Cool 20 minutes in pan. Remove rim; cut and serve
warm or cool. Refrigerate leftovers.

Makes 8 servings.

APPLE-RHUBARB TARTS

Top these little tartlets with sweetened whipped cream when serving.

2 cups fresh apples, peeled, cored and chopped
½ cup fresh rhubarb, chopped
½ cup water
½ teaspoon pure vanilla extract
¼ cup granulated sugar
⅛ teaspoon salt
1 tablespoon cornstarch, dissolved in 1 tablespoon cold water

pastry for a two-crust 9-inch pie, purchased or homemade

Preheat oven to 450°.
Mix apples, rhubarb, water, vanilla, sugar and salt in a saucepan. Cover and simmer until tender, about 8 to 10 minutes. Stir in cornstarch mixture; cook and stir until thickened; remove from heat; cool.

Press about 1 tablespoon pastry each into twenty 2½-inch tartlet pans; prick with fork. Bake until browned, about 10 minutes. Remove from oven; cool in pans, then remove from pans. Place a spoonful of fruit mixture into each shell when serving. Refrigerate leftovers.

Makes 20 tartlets.

APRICOT-GLAZED RHUBARB TART

Top with sweetened whipped cream when serving.

Crust
1 cup all-purpose flour mixed
    with 1 tablespoon granulated
    sugar and ¼ teaspoon salt
¾ cup cold butter, cut up
2 tablespoons cold water,
    approximately

Filling
4¼ cups fresh rhubarb,
    cut into ¼-inch slices
¼ cup granulated sugar
1 teaspoon pure vanilla extract
¼ cup apricot preserves, melted
    and strained

Almond mixture
¼ cup whole blanched almonds, finely ground
2 tablespoons granulated sugar
2 tablespoons all-purpose flour

Preheat oven to 375°.
Crust: Place flour mixture in a bowl; cut in butter with a pastry blender to coarse meal-like crumbs. Stir in water a little at a time with a fork until dough holds together. Form into a ball, then roll out into a flat disk. Wrap in food plastic wrap and chill 1 hour. Roll dough out between sheets of waxed paper into a 12-inch round; chill until firm. Remove top sheets of waxed paper and invert dough onto a large baking sheet; remove other sheet of waxed paper. Fold edge of crust in to form a ½-inch border, pressing to seal to bottom crust. Combine almond mixture ingredients and spread over crust bottom.

Filling: Fill crust with rhubarb. Sprinkle with granulated sugar, and drizzle with vanilla extract. Bake 35–45 minutes. Cool on baking on a rack. Brush rhubarb with apricot preserves to coat. Refrigerate leftovers.

Makes 8 servings.

BLACKBERRY-RHUBARB FOOL TART

A nice dessert.

Crust
1⅓ cups all-purpose flour
¼ teaspoon salt
½ cup cold butter, cut up
4 tablespoons ice water

1 pint fresh blackberries

Fool
2 cups fresh rhubarb, cut
into 1-inch pieces
½ cup granulated sugar
1 tablespoon fresh lemon juice
½ teaspoon pure vanilla extract
1 cup whipping cream, whipped
with 1 tablespoon powdered sugar

Crust: Mix flour and salt in a large bowl. Cut in butter with a pastry blender, or two knives, to coarse crumbs. Stir in water, 1 tablespoon at a time, and gently mix just until a ball can be formed. Press ball into a flat disk and wrap in food plastic wrap; refrigerate 30 minutes.

Preheat oven to 350°.
Roll out dough to ⅛-inch thickness, and place into a tart baking pan. Trim edges. Cover crust loosely with parchment paper, and weight down with pie weights or dried beans. Bake 15–20 minutes or until golden brown. Remove from oven; cool completely in pan.

Fool: Place rhubarb, granulated sugar and lemon juice in a saucepan. Cook over medium heat, stirring often, until rhubarb is very soft, about 15 minutes. Stir in vanilla. Puree mixture in food processor; refrigerate until cold. Fold cold puree into whipped cream, then refrigerate several hours. Spoon fool into baked crust about an hour before serving. Top fool evenly with the blackberries. Serve. Refrigerate leftovers.

Makes 6 servings.

BLUEBERRY-RHUBARB TART

Garnish this colorful red and blue tart with sweetened whipped cream.

Crust
1 cup all-purpose flour
1 tablespoon granulated sugar
¼ teaspoon salt
¼ cup butter
¼ cup solid shortening
3 tablespoons cold water

Filling
½ cup granulated sugar
3 tablespoons cornstarch
⅔ cup apple juice
2 cups fresh rhubarb, cut
　into ¼-inch pieces
1 teaspoon pure vanilla extract
1 cup blueberries

Preheat oven to 375°.
Crust: Stir flour, sugar and salt in a medium bowl. Cut in butter and shortening until crumbly. With a fork, stir in water, just until moistened; shape into a ball. Roll ball out on a lightly floured surface into a 10-inch circle. Place in a 9-inch tart baking pan with removable bottom; press dough on bottom and up sides of pan. Bake 10 minutes.

Filling: Place sugar and cornstarch in a saucepan. Gradually stir in apple juice. Stir in rhubarb. Cook over medium heat, stirring constantly, until thickened, about 7 minutes. Remove from heat; stir in vanilla and blueberries. Pour mixture into prepared crust. Bake 40–50 minutes or until center is bubbly. Cool completely before cutting. Refrigerate leftovers.

Makes 8 servings.

RASPBERRY-RHUBARB TART

Raspberries and red rhubarb…pretty as a picture.

Crust
2¼ cups all-purpose flour
1 teaspoon granulated sugar
¼ teaspoon salt
¾ cup cold butter, cut into
  small pieces
½ cup ice cold water

Filling
6 cups fresh red rhubarb,
  cut into 1-inch pieces
1 cup fresh raspberries
1 cup granulated sugar
3 tablespoons all-purpose flour
1 teaspoon pure vanilla extract

melted butter
1 tablespoon granulated sugar

Preheat oven to 400°.
Crust: Mix flour, sugar and salt in a bowl; cut in butter until mixture resembles coarse crumbs. Stir in water with a fork, and mix just until dough holds together. Form dough into a ball; cover with plastic food wrap; chill 30 minutes. Roll out dough, on a lightly floured surface, to a 14-inch circle, about ⅛-inch thickness. Place on a parchment-lined baking sheet.

Filling: In a large glass bowl, mix all filling ingredients. Spoon mixture in center of crust, leaving a 2-inch border around outer edge. Fold edge of dough over the rhubarb mixture, making pleats as you fold. Brush edge of dough with melted butter, then sprinkle with sugar. Bake 45–55 minutes. Remove from oven; cool slightly before serving. Refrigerate leftovers.

Makes 8 servings.

RHUBARB CRUMB TART

If you are a raspberry fan, try using raspberry-flavored gelatin, and toss in a few fresh raspberries along with the rhubarb.

Crust
1 cup all-purpose flour
1 teaspoon baking powder
3 tablespoons powdered sugar
⅓ cup butter or margarine
1 egg, beaten
4 teaspoons milk

Topping
½ cup all-purpose flour
1 cup granulated sugar
⅓ cup butter, cut up

Filling
3 cups fresh rhubarb, diced
1 teaspoon pure vanilla extract
1 3-ounce package strawberry flavored gelatin dessert mix

Preheat oven to 350°.
Crust: Mix flour, baking powder and powdered sugar in a bowl; cut in butter until mixture resembles coarse crumbs. Stir in egg and milk; form dough into a ball; pat into a greased 11x7-inch baking pan.

Filling: Spoon rhubarb over crust; drizzle with vanilla, and sprinkle with gelatin mix.

Topping: Mix all topping ingredients in a bowl; sprinkle over rhubarb mixture. Bake 45–50 minutes. Cool until firm. Refrigerate leftovers.

Makes 12 servings.

RHUBARB CUSTARD TART

A nice dessert for company.

Crust
**1 refrigerated pie crust,
   softened as directed from
   package or homemade**

Filling
¾ cup granulated sugar
3 tablespoons all-purpose flour
½ cup heavy cream
2 tablespoons apricot or peach preserves
1 egg yolk, beaten
1 teaspoon pure vanilla extract
3 cups fresh rhubarb, sliced

Topping
½ cup all-purpose flour
½ cup brown sugar, packed
¼ cup quick-cooking oatmeal
¼ cup butter or margarine, softened

Preheat oven to 375°.
Crust: Prepare pie crust as directed on package for one-crust filled pie using a 9-inch tart baking pan with removable bottom. Press crust onto bottom and sides of pan. Trim edges if necessary.

Filling: In a large bowl, mix sugar and flour. Stir in cream, preserves, egg and vanilla until blended. Stir in rhubarb. Pour mixture into prepared crust.

Topping: In a bowl, mix flour, brown sugar and oatmeal; cut in butter until crumbly. Sprinkle over filling. Place a baking sheet below tart pan to catch drippings. Bake 40–50 minutes or until bubbly and topping is browned. Cool 20 minutes before serving. Refrigerate leftovers.

Makes 8 servings.

RHUBARB TART

Serve with a dollop of cinnamon-topped sweetened whipped cream.

Crust
1½ cups all-purpose flour
¾ cup brown sugar, packed
½ cup butter, cut up

Filling
2 cups fresh rhubarb, cut into ¼-inch slices
2 eggs
¾ cup granulated sugar
2 tablespoons all-purpose flour
¼ teaspoon salt
½ cup light cream (half & half)
1 teaspoon pure vanilla extract
¼ cup finely chopped walnuts mixed with reserved ½ cup crumbs

Preheat oven to 350°.
Crust: Butter a 9-inch springform baking pan. Mix flour and brown sugar in a bowl; cut in butter until crumbly. Reserve ½ cup mixture. Press remaining mixture onto bottom and 1½ inches up side of prepared pan. Bake until light brown, about 15 minutes. Remove from oven.

Filling: Spoon rhubarb over hot crust. In a bowl, beat eggs on high one minute. Beat in sugar, flour, salt, light cream and vanilla until blended. Pour mixture over rhubarb. Sprinkle top with walnut-crumb mixture. Bake 40–45 minutes or until a knife inserted in center comes out clean. Cool in pan 2 hours; run a metal spatula around tart. Remove side of pan. Serve or refrigerate. Refrigerate leftovers.

Makes 8 servings.

STRAWBERRY-RHUBARB TART

Serve this delicious tart chilled...recipe courtesy of Janice from Oak Harbor, WA.

Crust
½ cup butter, softened
3 tablespoons dark brown sugar, packed
½ cup toasted almonds, finely chopped
1 large egg, beaten
¼ teaspoon almond extract
1⅓ cups all-purpose flour

Custard
2 large egg yolks
3 tablespoons granulated sugar
2½ tablespoons cornstarch
1 teaspoon pure vanilla extract
⅔ cup milk, heated
4 tablespoons butter, room temperature

Filling
4 cups fresh rhubarb,
  cut into 1-inch pieces
¾ cup granulated sugar
¼ teaspoon salt
1 tablespoon plus 1 teaspoon
  cornstarch mixed in a cup
  with ¼ cup water

Topping
4 cups fresh strawberries
1 cup red currant jelly,
  melted and cooled

Preheat oven to 375°. Butter a 10-inch tart pan.
Crust: Beat butter and brown sugar in a bowl. Stir in nuts, egg and almond extract. Mix in flour. Press dough onto bottom and 2 inches up sides. Chill 30 minutes, then bake 15–20 minutes. Cool.

Custard: Beat first four ingredients in a medium saucepan until pale yellow. Gradually stir in milk to blend; stir over medium heat until thickened and smooth. Whisk in butter with wire whisk, a tablespoon at a time. Pour mixture into a bowl; cool, then cover and refrigerate.

Filling: Mix rhubarb, sugar and salt in a saucepan. Stir in cornstarch mixture; bring to a boil over medium heat, stirring constantly. Reduce heat to low; cover and simmer, stirring often, until rhubarb is tender, about 10 minutes; cool; refrigerate. Release crust from tart pan; pour cold custard into crust. Cover with rhubarb filling. Top with strawberries; brush with cooled melted jelly.

Makes 8 servings.

LEMON SHERBET-RHUBARB TORTE

A frosty lemon rhubarb torte.

Crust
3 cups blanched slivered
  almonds, toasted
½ cup granulated sugar
5 tablespoons margarine, melted
¼ teaspoon ground cinnamon
5 tablespoons strawberry
  preserves, melted
3 pints lemon sherbet,
  slightly softened

Sauce
1 cup granulated sugar
½ cup water
1 20-ounce bag frozen
  unsweetened rhubarb
1 teaspoon pure vanilla extract
1 20-ounce bag frozen
  unsweetened strawberries

1 pint fresh strawberries, hulled

Preheat oven to 350°.
Crust: Process almonds and sugar until finely chopped; place into a bowl.
Add margarine and cinnamon; mix well. Press mixture firmly onto bottom
and 2 inches up sides of a 9-inch springform baking pan. Place on a baking
sheet and bake 20 minutes. Remove from oven; cool completely in pan.
Spread melted preserves over bottom of crust. Top evenly with softened
sherbet. Freeze until firm.

Sauce: Bring sugar, water and rhubarb to a boil in a heavy saucepan over
high heat, stirring often. Reduce heat; cover and simmer until rhubarb is
tender, about 8 minutes. Stir in vanilla. Add frozen strawberries; bring to a
simmer. Remove from heat. Cool. Cover and chill well. When serving,
remove pan sides, and spoon ½ cup sauce over torte. Top with fresh
strawberries. Slice and serve with sauce. Freeze leftovers.

Makes 12 servings.

MALLOW-TOPPED RHUBARB TORTE

Marshmallows and pudding in this sweet rhubarb torte.

Crust
2 cups graham cracker crumbs
1½ tablespoons all-purpose flour
¼ cup granulated sugar
½ cup butter, melted

Topping
1½ cups miniature marshmallow
1 cup whipping cream, whipped
1 3-ounce package instant vanilla
pudding

Filling
4 cups rhubarb, sliced
1¼ cups granulated sugar mixed in a bowl with ¼ cup cornstarch
1 teaspoon pure vanilla extract

Preheat oven to 350°.
Crust: Mix all crust ingredients; press into an ungreased 13x9-inch baking pan. Bake 10 minutes. Remove from oven; cool.

Filling: Mix all filling ingredients in a saucepan; cook and stir over medium heat until thickened, about 4 minutes. Cool, then spread over crust.

Topping: Fold marshmallows into whipped cream; spread over rhubarb layer. Prepare pudding according to package directions; gently pour over marshmallow layer. Chill well. Refrigerate leftovers.

Makes 9 servings.

OLD-FASHIONED RHUBARB TORTE

A torte for all times.

Crust
1½ cups all-purpose flour
1 tablespoon granulated sugar
¾ cup butter, softened

Topping
6 egg whites
¾ cup granulated sugar
1 teaspoon pure vanilla extract

Filling
6 egg yolks
¼ cup all-purpose flour
1 cup evaporated milk
2 cups granulated sugar
8 cups fresh rhubarb, diced
1 teaspoon pure vanilla extract

Preheat oven to 350°.
Crust: In a bowl using an electric mixer, slowly beat flour, sugar and butter until blended; press mixture into a greased 13x9-inch baking pan. Bake 15 minutes. Cool.

Filling: In a bowl, stir egg yolks, flour, evaporated milk and sugar until blended; stir in rhubarb and vanilla. Pour mixture into prepared crust. Bake until set, about 1 hour.

Topping: In a large bowl, beat egg whites until foamy. Gradually beat in sugar and vanilla extract to stiff peaks. Spread meringue over rhubarb. Bake until light golden brown, about 15 minutes. Serve warm or cold. Refrigerate leftovers.

Makes 12 servings.

RHUBARB TORTE

A delicious torte…thanks to Lori Jones.

Crust
1 cup all-purpose flour
⅛ teaspoon salt
2 tablespoons granulated sugar
½ cup butter

Filling
¾ cup granulated sugar
2 tablespoons all-purpose flour
⅓ cup cream or milk
3 egg yolks
3 cups rhubarb, cut into ½-inch pieces
1 teaspoon pure vanilla extract

Topping
3 egg whites
¼ teaspoon cream of tartar
6 tablespoons granulated sugar

Preheat oven to 350°.
Crust: Mix flour, salt and sugar in a bowl; cut in butter until crumbly. Press mixture into a 9-inch torte baking pan. Bake 15 minutes; set aside.

Filling: In a saucepan, stir sugar, flour, cream and egg yolks until blended. Stir in rhubarb and vanilla; cook, over medium heat, stirring often, until rhubarb is tender. Pour mixture into baked crust.

Topping: Beat egg whites in a bowl until foamy. Beat in cream of tartar and sugar to stiff peaks. Spread over rhubarb; bake until golden brown, about 10–15 minutes. Serve at room temperature. Refrigerate leftovers.

Makes 8 servings.

Muffins
Breads

APPLESAUCE-RHUBARB MUFFINS

Applesauce and rhubarb...a moist muffin.

Dry ingredients
2 cups all-purpose flour
1 cup whole wheat flour
2 teaspoons baking powder
½ teaspoon baking soda
½ teaspoon salt
2 teaspoons ground cinnamon

Wet ingredients
2 eggs, beaten
1 teaspoon pure vanilla extract
1¼ cups brown sugar, packed
1¼ cups sweetened applesauce
½ cup corn oil
**1½ cups fresh rhubarb,
   finely chopped**

Topping
granulated sugar

Preheat oven to 400°.
Dry: Mix all dry ingredients in a large bowl.

Wet: In another bowl, mix all wet ingredients except rhubarb; add to dry ingredients. Fold in rhubarb. Stir only to moisten. Spoon into lightly greased or paper-lined muffin pan, filling each cup ⅔ full.

Topping: Sprinkle tops with granulated sugar. Bake 20–25 minutes. Remove from pan and cool on a wire rack. Serve warm.

Makes 24 muffins.

CINNAMON RHUBARB MUFFINS

Butter and sour cream give this rhubarb muffin a special texture.

½ cup brown sugar, packed
¼ cup butter, softened
1 cup dairy sour cream
2 eggs
1 teaspoon pure vanilla extract

1½ cups all-purpose flour
¾ teaspoon baking soda
½ teaspoon ground cinnamon
1½ cups fresh rhubarb, cut into ¼-inch slices

1 tablespoon granulated sugar mixed with ½ teaspoon
  ground cinnamon

Preheat oven to 375°.
Beat brown sugar and butter in a bowl on medium speed until creamy. Add sour cream, eggs and vanilla extract; beat until well mixed.

In a bowl, mix flour, baking soda and cinnamon; stir mixture into creamed mixture by hand just until moistened. Stir in rhubarb. Spoon into a greased or paper-lined 12-cup muffin pan.

Sprinkle tops equally with granulated sugar mixture. Bake 25–30 minutes. Let stand 5 minutes, then remove from pan. Cool on a wire rack.

Makes 12 muffins.

OAT BRAN RHUBARB MUFFINS

Cholesterol-free recipe adapted from my book *The Muffins are Coming*.

Dry ingredients
1½ cups all-purpose flour
½ cup oat bran
2 teaspoons baking powder
½ teaspoon baking soda
½ teaspoon salt
¾ cup brown sugar, packed
½ teaspoon ground cinnamon
1 tablespoon non-fat dry milk
½ cup walnuts, chopped

Wet ingredients
2 egg whites, beaten with
**   1 teaspoon corn oil**
½ cup buttermilk
⅓ cup corn oil
1 teaspoon pure vanilla extract
1 cup fresh rhubarb, finely cut

Preheat oven to 325°. Grease or line a muffin pan with paper baking cups.

In a large bowl, combine all dry ingredients; mix well.

In a medium bowl, combine all wet ingredients; mix well.

Combine dry and wet ingredients. Stir only to moisten; batter will be lumpy. Spoon batter into prepared muffin pan. Bake 25–30 minutes. Remove from pan and cool on a rack. Serve warm with honey.

Makes 12 muffins.

ORANGE-RHUBARB MUFFINS

Serve warm with strawberry-rhubarb jam.

Dry ingredients
2 cups all-purpose flour
¾ cup granulated sugar
1½ teaspoons baking powder
½ teaspoon baking soda
½ teaspoon salt
¾ cup pecans, chopped

1 large egg, beaten
¼ cup corn oil
2 teaspoons freshly grated orange peel
¾ cup fresh orange juice
1 teaspoon pure vanilla extract
1¼ cups fresh rhubarb, finely chopped

Preheat oven to 350°.
In a large bowl, combine all dry ingredients.

Mix remaining ingredients in another bowl until blended; stir into flour mixture just until moistened. Spoon batter into greased or paper-lined muffin pan. Bake 25–30 minutes. Remove from pan; cool on a rack.

Makes about 12 muffins.

RHUBARB HONEY MUFFINS

A taste of honey…serve these muffins warm with cinnamon-butter.

Dry ingredients
2½ cups all-purpose flour
1 teaspoon baking soda
½ teaspoon salt

1 egg, beaten
1 cup brown sugar, packed
⅔ cup corn oil
½ cup honey
1 teaspoon pure vanilla extract
¾ cup buttermilk
1½ cups fresh rhubarb, finely chopped
½ cup pecans, chopped

1 tablespoon butter, mixed with
** ½ cup granulated sugar until crumbly**

Preheat oven to 350°. Paper-line muffin pans.
In a large bowl, mix all dry ingredients.

In another bowl, stir egg, brown sugar, corn oil, honey, vanilla extract and buttermilk until blended; stir into flour mixture just until moistened. Fold in rhubarb and pecans. Fill muffin cups about ⅔ full.

Sprinkle tops with butter-sugar mixture. Bake 25–35 minutes or until golden. Remove from pan; cool on a rack.

Makes 24 muffins.

RHUBARB-STRAWBERRY MUFFINS

Serve warm with softened butter.

1¾ cups all-purpose flour
½ cup granulated sugar
2 teaspoons baking powder
½ teaspoon salt

1 egg, beaten
¾ cup whole milk
⅓ cup corn oil
1 cup fresh rhubarb, finely chopped
½ cup fresh strawberries, sliced
2 teaspoons grated orange rind

granulated sugar

Preheat oven to 400°.
In a large bowl, mix together first four ingredients.

In another bowl mix egg, milk and oil to blend; stir into first bowl mixture.
Stir in rhubarb, strawberries and orange rind just until moistened. Spoon
into greased or paper-lined 12-cup muffin pan.

Sprinkle tops lightly with granulated sugar. Bake 20–25 minutes or until a
wooden pick inserted in center comes out clean. Remove from pan; cool
on a wire rack.

Makes 12 muffins.

RHUBARB WHEAT BRAN MUFFINS

Serve warm with soften butter and honey.

1 cup all-bran dry cereal
1 cup buttermilk
1 egg, beaten
½ cup corn oil

1½ cups all-purpose flour
¾ cup brown sugar
1 teaspoon baking soda
½ teaspoon salt
1½ cups fresh rhubarb, diced

2 tablespoons granulated sugar mixed
   with ½ teaspoon ground cinnamon

Preheat oven to 400°.
Mix cereal and buttermilk in a bowl; let stand a few minutes to soften cereal.
Stir in egg and oil.

Mix flour, brown sugar, baking soda and salt in another bowl; stir into first mixture only to moisten. Stir in rhubarb. Spoon batter into greased or paper-lined muffin pan. Sprinkle tops with sugar-cinnamon mixture. Bake 25–28 minutes. Remove from pan; cool on a rack. Serve warm. Refrigerate leftovers.

Makes 12 muffins.

APPLE-RHUBARB BREAD

Serve plain or with softened butter.

1½ cups fresh rhubarb, finely chopped
1½ cups apples, peeled and finely chopped
1½ cups granulated sugar
⅔ cup corn oil
2 teaspoons pure vanilla extract
4 eggs

3 cups all-purpose flour
2 teaspoons baking powder
½ teaspoon baking soda
1 teaspoon salt
1 teaspoon ground cinnamon
½ teaspoon ground cloves
½ cup nuts, coarsely chopped

Preheat oven to 350°.
Grease bottoms only of two 9x5x3-inch loaf pans.

Mix rhubarb, apples, sugar, oil, vanilla and eggs in a large bowl. In another bowl, mix remaining ingredients; stir into the first mixture. Pour batter into prepared pans. Bake 50–60 minutes or until a wooden pick inserted in center comes out clean. Remove from oven; cool 10 minutes in pan. Loosen edges of loaves from pans; remove to a wire rack. Cool completely before slicing. Wrap in food plastic wrap; store in refrigerator for up to 10 days.

Makes 2 loaves.

ORANGE-RHUBARB BREAD

Wrap and store in refrigerator. Wait a day before serving for a more intense flavor...if you can wait.

½ cup granulated sugar
⅔ cup shortening
2 eggs

2 cups all-purpose flour
1 teaspoon baking powder
½ teaspoon baking soda
1 teaspoon salt
¼ teaspoon ground nutmeg
½ cup fresh orange juice, mixed with ½ teaspoon vanilla
1 cup rhubarb, finely cut
½ cup pecans, chopped
1 tablespoon freshly grated orange peel

Preheat oven to 350°.
Grease bottom only of a 9x5x3-inch loaf pan. Beat sugar and shortening in a bowl until creamy. Beat in eggs, one at a time.

Mix flour, baking powder, soda, salt and nutmeg in a bowl; stir in sugar-egg mixture alternately with orange juice mixture. Stir in pecans and orange peel. Pour batter into prepared pan; let stand 20 minutes at room temperature. Bake about 1 hour or until a wooden pick inserted in center comes out clean. Cool completely on a rack.

Makes 1 loaf.

PECAN RHUBARB BREAD

You may use fresh or frozen rhubarb…if using frozen, do not thaw.

¾ cup granulated sugar
½ cup butter or margarine, softened
2 eggs
1 cup buttermilk
½ teaspoon pure vanilla extract

2 cups all-purpose flour
½ teaspoon baking powder
½ teaspoon baking soda
¼ teaspoon salt
½ cup toasted chopped pecans, cooled

1 cup rhubarb, sliced
1 tablespoon granulated sugar, mixed with pinch of ground cinnamon

Preheat oven to 350°.
Grease bottom only of a 9x5-inch loaf pan. Beat sugar and butter in a large bowl until fluffy. Beat in eggs, one at a time. Stir in buttermilk and vanilla.

In a bowl, mix flour, baking powder, soda, salt and pecans. Stir into first mixture just until moistened.

Fold in rhubarb. Pour batter into prepared pan. Sprinkle sugar-cinnamon mixture over top.

Bake 50–60 minutes or until wooden pick inserted in center comes out clean. Cool 15 minutes. Remove from pan. Cool completely on wire rack. Wrap and store in refrigerator.

Makes 1 loaf.

RHUBARB BREAD

This bread will produce about 20 slices per loaf.

1½ cups brown sugar, packed
⅔ cup corn oil
1 egg
1 teaspoon pure vanilla extract

2½ cups all-purpose flour
1 teaspoon salt
1 teaspoon baking soda
½ teaspoon ground cinnamon
1 cup buttermilk
2 cups rhubarb, diced
½ cup chopped nuts

1 tablespoon butter, softened
¼ cup granulated sugar

Preheat oven to 350°.
Grease two 8x4-inch loaf pans. Beat brown sugar and oil in a bowl until creamy. Beat in egg. Add vanilla.

In a bowl, mix flour, salt, soda and cinnamon. Stir sugar-oil mixture into bowl, alternately with buttermilk, until dry ingredients are moist. Fold in rhubarb and nuts.

Pour batter into prepared pans. Mix butter and granulated sugar; sprinkle over batter. Bake 50–55 minutes or until wooden pick inserted in centers comes out clean. Cool in pan 10 minutes. Remove from pan; cool completely on a wire rack. Wrap and store in refrigerator.

Makes 2 loaves.

RHUBARB QUICK BREAD

If you don't have buttermilk on hand…stir 1 tablespoon fresh lemon juice or white vinegar into 1 cup whole milk.

1½ cups brown sugar
⅔ cup corn oil
1 egg

2½ cups all-purpose flour
1 teaspoon salt
1 teaspoon baking soda

1 cup buttermilk, mixed with
    1 tablespoon fresh lemon juice
    and 1 teaspoon pure vanilla extract
1½ cups rhubarb, diced
½ cup walnuts, chopped

¼ cup brown sugar, packed and mixed
    with ½ teaspoon ground
    cinnamon
1 tablespoon butter, melted

Preheat oven to 350°.
Grease two 9x5x3-inch loaf pans. In a large bowl, beat sugar and oil until creamy. Beat in egg.

Mix flour, salt and baking soda in a bowl; stir into sugar-oil mixture, alternately with buttermilk mixture. Fold in rhubarb and walnuts. Pour batter into prepared pans.

In a small bowl, mix brown sugar-cinnamon and melted butter; sprinkle over top of each loaf.

Bake about 40 minutes or until a wooden pick inserted in centers comes out clean. Cool completely on a rack. Wrap and store in refrigerator.

Makes 2 loaves.

RHUBARB TEA BREAD

Serve warm with strawberry-rhubarb jam for a tasty treat.

3 eggs
1 cup corn oil
2 cups brown sugar, packed
2 teaspoons pure vanilla extract
2½ cups fresh rhubarb, finely chopped
½ cup walnuts, chopped

3 cups all-purpose flour
2 teaspoons baking soda
½ teaspoon baking powder
¾ teaspoon salt
2 teaspoons ground cinnamon
½ teaspoon ground nutmeg
½ teaspoon allspice

Preheat oven to 350°.
Grease two 9x5-inch loaf pans.

In a large bowl, beat eggs, oil, sugar and vanilla until thick and foamy. Stir in rhubarb and nuts. Mix remaining ingredients in another bowl; stir into creamed mixture until well-blended. Spoon batter into prepared pans. Bake about 60 minutes or until a wooden pick inserted in centers comes out clean. Cool in pan 10 minutes. Remove and cool on a rack. Wrap in plastic food wrap and store in refrigerator.

Makes 2 loaves.

STREUSEL RHUBARB BREAD

Flavor will improve the second day…perfect to make ahead for special company.

1 cup granulated sugar
½ cup butter, softened
⅓ cup fresh orange juice
½ teaspoon pure vanilla extract
2 large eggs

2 cups all-purpose flour
1 teaspoon baking powder
¼ teaspoon baking soda
¼ teaspoon salt
1½ cups fresh rhubarb, cut into ¼-inch pieces

Streusel
2 tablespoon granulated sugar
2 tablespoons brown sugar, packed
1 tablespoon all-purpose flour
1½ teaspoon ground cinnamon
1 tablespoon butter, melted

Preheat oven to 350°.
Grease and flour an 8x4-inch loaf pan. Beat sugar and butter in a bowl until creamy. Add orange juice, vanilla and eggs; beat just until mixed.

Mix flour, baking powder, baking soda and salt in another bowl; by hand, stir into first bowl just until moistened. Fold in rhubarb. Reserve 1½ cups batter. Pour remaining batter into prepared pan.

Stir all streusel ingredients in a bowl until crumbly; sprinkle half of mixture over batter in pan. Press lightly into batter. Carefully spread reserved batter into pan. Top with remaining streusel mixture; press into batter.

Bake 65–70 minutes or until a wooden pick inserted in center comes out clean. Cool 10 minutes; remove from pan. Cool completely. Store wrapped in refrigerator.

Makes 1 loaf or about 12 servings.

Main Meals Paired with Rhubarb

CORNISH HENS WITH RHUBARB SAUCE

Offer warm bread to complete the meal.

3 Cornish game hens, cut in half
corn oil
salt and ground black pepper,
 to taste

4 cups fresh rhubarb,
 cut into ½-inch slices
1 cup tomato-style barbecue sauce
¼ cup water

8 ounces dried orzo (pasta)
1 tablespoon butter
1 cup fresh carrots, shredded
½ cup green onions, sliced
1 tablespoon flat parsley,
 chopped

mixed salad greens
cherry tomatoes, halved

Preheat oven to 375°.
Coat top and inside of each hen with oil. Sprinkle with salt and black pepper.
Arrange hens, cut-side down, in a greased 15x10x1-inch baking pan.
Bake uncovered 40 minutes.

Bring rhubarb, barbecue sauce, and water to a boil in a saucepan, then
reduce heat to medium-low. Cover and cook 20 minutes, stirring often.
Remove from heat. Stir to mash rhubarb slightly. Reserve 1 cup sauce.
Brush the top of hens with some of the remaining sauce, and continue
baking 20 minutes, brushing with sauce until hens are tender and no
longer pink, and an instant-read cooking thermometer inserted in thigh
registers 180°.

Cook orzo following package directions; drain. Place in a large bowl; stir in
butter. Stir in 1 cup reserved sauce, carrots, green onions and parsley. To
serve, arrange salad greens on individual dinner plates; spoon center with a
portion of orzo mixture; top with one hen half. Garnish with tomatoes. Heat
and serve remaining sauce.

Makes 6 servings.

DUCK BREAST WITH RHUBARB SAUCE

Serve with garlic mashed potatoes and steamed sugar snap peas.

½ cup port wine
½ cup dried cherries

2 duck breasts, about
1 pound each
Salt and finely ground
black pepper to taste

¼ cup chopped shallots
4 cups fresh rhubarb, cut into
½-inch pieces
1½ cups chicken stock

1 tablespoon arrowroot dissolved in
2 tablespoons fresh orange juice
1 teaspoon coarsely ground black pepper
salt to taste

Preheat oven to 400°.
Heat port wine in a small saucepan until hot. Add cherries; cover and let stand
15 minutes.

Score the skin of the duck in a cross pattern; season both sides with salt and
pepper. Heat a medium skillet over high heat until very hot; place duck skin
side down in skillet. Reduce heat to medium-low. Cook, removing fat from
skillet as it accumulates. Place duck breasts in a small roasting pan. Roast in
oven about 10 minutes for medium rare, or longer as desired. Remove from
oven; let rest 10 minutes before slicing. Slice at an angle.

Leave 2 tablespoons fat in skillet; add shallots; cook and stir until softened.
Add rhubarb; cook and stir 5 minutes. Spoon mixture into a bowl. Add cherry-
port wine mixture to skillet; simmer 1 minute. Add chicken stock; simmer until
reduced by a third.

Whisk in the arrowroot mixture, and bring sauce to a boil. Stir in coarsely
ground black pepper. Add salt to taste. Simmer sauce until thickened.
Add the shallot-rhubarb mixture to sauce; heat thoroughly.

Divide sliced roasted duck breasts among 4 plates. Serve each portion with
rhubarb sauce. Refrigerate leftovers.

Makes 4 servings.

GRILLED CHICKEN WITH RHUBARB RELISH

Serve with warm hard rolls and crisp green salad.

Relish
3 cups fresh rhubarb, diced
¾ cup granulated sugar
1 tablespoon freshly grated orange zest
1 cup fresh orange juice
1 jalapeno pepper, seeded and chopped
2 shallots, minced

Chicken
6 boneless skinless chicken breast halves
corn oil
1 tablespoon fresh lemon juice
salt
ground black pepper

Relish: Bring all relish ingredients to a boil in a saucepan, then reduce heat and simmer, stirring often, until mixture thickens, about 10 minutes. Cool; set aside.

Chicken: Preheat grill. Brush chicken with corn oil and lemon juice. Sprinkle salt and pepper to taste. Grill about 6 minutes per side, or until chicken is no longer pink and juices run clear. Serve immediately with rhubarb relish. Refrigerate leftovers.

Makes 6 servings.

HAM WITH RHUBARB CHUTNEY

Serve with rice pilaf and salad greens.

2 teaspoons yellow mustard seeds
2 cups fresh rhubarb, cut into ½ -inch pieces
1 cup chopped red onion
½ cup water
½ cup cherry preserves
½ cup dried cranberries
6 tablespoons granulated sugar
4 teaspoons balsamic vinegar

salt and ground black pepper to taste
2 13-ounce fully cooked ham steaks, quartered

Place the mustard seeds in a medium saucepan. Toast over medium heat 2 minutes. Add remaining ingredients except salt and pepper and ham steaks. Simmer until rhubarb is tender, about 5 minutes. Bring to a boil; cook and stir until mixture thickens, about 5 minutes. Season with salt and pepper to taste.

Preheat broiler.
Place ham on a baking sheet; broil until brown on the edges, about 3 minutes. Do not turn ham. Serve immediately with chutney. Refrigerate leftovers.

Makes 4 servings.

LENTILS CURRIED WITH RHUBARB

Serve this vegetarian dish hot with cooked brown rice. Garnish with shredded coconut.

1 cup dried orange-colored lentils
1 large sweet potato, peeled and sliced

1 tablespoon corn oil
1 cup fresh rhubarb, diced
2 tablespoons liquid sweetener
1 tablespoon curry powder
1 teaspoon freshly grated ginger root
1 teaspoon hot red chili powder
salt and ground black pepper to taste

Cover lentils with water in a deep pot. Bring to a boil, then reduce heat and add sweet potato slices. Simmer until soft, about 1 hour. Remove from heat; drain; mash with a fork and set aside.

Preheat oven to 400°.
Heat corn oil in a skillet until hot. Add rhubarb; stir and cook until tender. Stir in sweetener and seasonings; add to mashed lentils. Pour into a glass baking dish. Bake until very hot, about 20 minutes. Refrigerate leftovers.

Makes 4 servings.

PORK LOIN WITH RHUBARB SAUCE

Serve with hot cooked flavored rice along with buttered asparagus, a crisp garden salad and onion rolls with butter.

1 3-pound boneless top pork loin roast (single loin), fat trimmed
¼ cup Dijon-style mustard
2 tablespoons minced garlic
½ teaspoon salt
½ teaspoon ground black pepper

Sauce
3 cups fresh rhubarb, cut into ½-inch pieces
1 tablespoon fresh onion, minced
⅓ cup fresh orange juice
1 tablespoon cider vinegar
6 tablespoons granulated sugar
¼ teaspoon salt

Preheat oven to 325°.
Score top and bottom of roast with a sharp knife in a diamond pattern, with cuts ¼-inch deep. Mix mustard, garlic, salt and pepper in a bowl; rub onto all sides of meat. Insert a meat thermometer near center of roast. Place roast on a rack in a shallow baking pan. Roast 1¼–1¾ hours or until meat thermometer registers 155°. Remove roast to a platter; cover with foil and let rest 15 minutes before slicing.

Bring all sauce ingredients to a boil in a saucepan. Reduce heat; cover and simmer 15 minutes, stirring often. Serve warm with roast.

Makes 8 servings.

PORK STEW WITH RHUBARB

Serve with warm crusty bread.

¼ cup corn oil
¼ cup all-purpose flour
1 teaspoon curry powder
½ teaspoon salt
¼ teaspoon ground black pepper
1½ pounds pork stew meat

1 cup onion, chopped
1 large clove garlic, chopped
1½ cups apple cider
1 cup water
4 cups fresh rhubarb, diced
1 tablespoon honey

Heat corn oil in a heavy saucepan. Mix flour, curry powder, salt and pepper in a bowl; coat pork with mixture; shake off excess into bowl, and reserve flour. Add coated pork to saucepan; brown well. Add onion and garlic to saucepan; cook and stir 1 minute. Add cider, water and rhubarb. Cover and simmer until meat is tender, about 1 hour. Stir in honey. Take 1 cup liquid from saucepan, and stir into reserved flour in bowl until thickened. Stir paste into stew; cook 8 minutes. Adjust seasonings if necessary.

Makes 4 servings.

PORK WITH RHUBARB CHUTNEY

Serve with buttered parsley-rice.

Rhubarb chutney
¾ cup granulated sugar
⅓ cup cider vinegar
1 tablespoon fresh ginger,
 minced and peeled
1 tablespoon ground fresh garlic
1 teaspoon cumin
½ teaspoon ground cinnamon
½ teaspoon ground cloves
¼ teaspoon dried crushed red pepper
4 cups fresh rhubarb, cut into ½-inch pieces
½ cup red onion, chopped
⅓ cup dried tart cherries
2 tablespoons golden raisins

Pork
2 1-pound pork tenderloins,
 trimmed of fat, seasoned
 to taste with salt and
 ground black pepper
2 teaspoons ground cumin
1 tablespoon olive oil

Preheat oven to 400°.
Rhubarb chutney: Mix first eight chutney ingredients in a heavy saucepan.
Bring to a simmer over low heat, stirring until sugar is dissolved. Add
rhubarb, onion, dried cherries and raisins. Cook over medium heat until
rhubarb is tender and mixture is slightly thickened, about 5 minutes. Cool.

Pork: Sprinkle pork with cumin. Heat oil in a large heavy skillet over high
heat. Add pork; brown all sides. Place in a roasting pan. Brush pork with
6 tablespoons chutney. Roast until a cooking thermometer inserted into
center of pork registers 155°, about 25 minutes, brushing occasionally with
6 more tablespoons chutney. Remove pork to serving platter; slice into
medallions. Serve with remaining chutney.

Makes 4 servings.

RHUBARB-GLAZED BABY BACK RIBS

Serve with a pasta salad and green salad along with warm rolls.

Rhubarb glaze
5 cups fresh rhubarb, sliced
1 12-ounce can frozen
   cranberry-apple juice concentrate
2 tablespoons cornstarch dissolved
   in 2 tablespoons water
⅓ cup honey
2 tablespoons Dijon-style mustard
1 tablespoon wine vinegar

Ribs
3 pounds pork loin-back ribs
½ teaspoon onion salt
½ teaspoon ground black pepper

Rhubarb glaze: Bring rhubarb and frozen juice to a boil in a saucepan.
Reduce heat; cover and simmer 15 minutes or until rhubarb is very soft.
Strain, pressing out liquid with back of a large spoon to measure 1¼ cups.
Discard pulp. Return liquid to same saucepan. Stir in cornstarch mixture;
stir and cook until thickened; continue cooking 2 minutes. Stir in honey,
mustard and wine vinegar. Heat thoroughly. Use the half the glaze for
grilling, and reserve other half for serving with cooked ribs.

Ribs: Cut ribs into serving pieces. Cover ribs with water in a large pot.
Bring to a boil over high heat, then reduce heat. Cover and simmer 30
minutes. Drain ribs. Season with onion salt and black pepper. To grill ribs in
a covered grill, arrange preheated coals around a drip pan. Test for medium
heat above drip pan. Place precooked ribs on grill rack over drip pan. Cover
and grill 45–50 minutes or until ribs are tender, brushing occasionally with
rhubarb glaze during last 10 minutes of grilling. Serve hot. Heat reserved
glaze and serve with ribs.

Makes 4 servings.

RHUBARB PORK CHOP CASSEROLE

Serve with steamed broccoli and hard rolls with butter.

1 tablespoon corn oil
4 pork loin chops, ¾-inch thick, seasoned to taste
   with salt and ground black pepper
3 cups soft bread crumbs

3 cups fresh rhubarb, cut into 1-inch pieces
½ cup brown sugar
¼ cup all-purpose flour
¾ teaspoon ground cinnamon

Preheat oven to 350°.
Heat corn oil in a large skillet. Add pork chops; brown on both sides.
Remove from skillet; set aside. Mix ¼ cup pan drippings with bread crumbs;
reserve ½ cup. Spoon remaining crumbs into a 13x9-inch glass baking
dish.

Mix rhubarb, sugar, flour and cinnamon in a bowl; spoon half over bread
crumbs. Place pork chops on top. Spoon remaining rhubarb mixture over
chops. Cover with cooking foil, and bake 30–45 minutes. Remove foil.
Sprinkle with reserved bread crumbs. Continue baking 15 minutes or until
pork chops test done. Refrigerate leftovers.

Makes 4 servings.

SHORT RIBS IN RHUBARB BBQ SAUCE

Serve with buttered long grain white rice and a side of steamed kale.

4 pounds lean, meaty beef short ribs
½ cup water
½ teaspoon seasoned salt

Sauce
1 cup fresh rhubarb, sliced
1 envelope onion soup mix (1½-ounce)
⅓ cup honey
⅓ cup chili sauce
¾ cup rose` wine
⅓ cup water
½ teaspoon dried basil
⅛ teaspoon ground black pepper

Red onion, sliced

Preheat oven to 350°.
Place ribs in a greased 13x9-inch baking pan. Add water. Sprinkle with seasoned salt. Cover with cooking foil. Bake two hours.

Sauce: Simmer all ingredients in a saucepan 30 minutes. Pour over ribs (after they have baked for 2 hours) and continue baking uncovered 30 minutes, basting often. Place on a serving platter; garnish with red onion slices. Serve hot.

Makes 6 servings.

SMOTHERED CHICKEN WITH RHUBARB

Serve this Cajun-like dish over hot long grain rice along with a crisp green salad and a side of boiled okra.

¼ cup corn oil
1 3-pound chicken, cut into serving pieces, seasoned to taste with
salt, ground black pepper, ground red pepper, ground paprika,
dried oregano and crushed thyme
1 tablespoon all-purpose flour

4 cups fresh rhubarb, cut into ½-inch pieces
2 medium onions, chopped
1 tablespoon fresh garlic, chopped
1 cup white wine
water, if needed
3 tablespoons parsley, finely chopped

Heat oil in a large heavy saucepan until hot. Add chicken; sprinkle with flour. Brown chicken 6 minutes on each side. Add rhubarb and onions; cook and stir until onions are browned. Add garlic; cook and stir 1 minute. Add wine. Cover and cook over medium-low heat 45 minutes, stirring often, or until chicken is tender. Add water if chicken seems too dry. Stir in parsley. Serve or refrigerate.

Makes 6 servings.

TURKEY WITH RHUBARB SAUCE

Serve with stove top dressing, buttered peas and warm soft rolls.

2 cups fresh rhubarb, chopped
3 tablespoons granulated sugar
2 tablespoons water
1 tablespoon frozen orange juice concentrate, thawed
½ teaspoon finely shredded fresh orange peel
1 2½-pound fresh bone-in turkey breast half, skin removed,
 seasoned to taste with salt and ground black pepper

Preheat oven to 375°.
Bring rhubarb, sugar, water, orange juice and orange peel to a boil in a saucepan. Reduce heat; cover and simmer 5 minutes or until rhubarb is tender. Cool; set aside.

Place turkey on a rack in a shallow roasting pan. Spread ¼ cup sauce over turkey. Roast 40 minutes. Spread ¼ cup sauce over turkey. Insert a meat thermometer into the thickest part of turkey breast without touching the bone. Continue cooking 35 minutes or until thermometer registers 175°. Let stand covered 10 minutes before slicing. Heat remaining rhubarb sauce; serve with turkey.

Makes 6 servings.

Soups
Salads

MINTED RHUBARB SOUP

A beautiful dessert soup...courtesy of my cousin Jane.

1½ cups white grape juice
¼ cup granulated sugar
5 sprigs fresh mint
1½ pounds rhubarb, cut into 1-inch pieces
1 pint fresh raspberries

½ cup mascarpone cheese
1 tablespoon powdered sugar

Bring grape juice and granulated sugar to a gentle boil over moderate heat, in a nonreactive saucepan; stir until sugar is dissolved. Remove from heat. Add mint leaves; let stand 15 minutes. Remove mint. Bring juice to a boil. Add rhubarb; simmer until soft, about 10 minutes. Reduce heat to low. Add raspberries; simmer 5 minutes. Remove from heat; cool. Puree mixture, and strain through a sieve into a bowl. Cover and chill for at least 2 hours.

Whip the cheese and powdered sugar in a bowl until thickened. Serve soup in chilled bowls. Top with a dollop of whipped mascarpone. Garnish with fresh raspberries and mint. Refrigerate leftovers.

Makes 4 servings.

COLD STRAWBERRY-RHUBARB SOUP

Garnish cold soup with sour cream and whole strawberries.

3 cups rhubarb, cut into ½-inch pieces
3 cups water
¾ cup granulated sugar
1 teaspoon grated orange peel
1 cup strawberries
⅓ cup dry white wine

Bring rhubarb, water, sugar and orange peel to a boil in a saucepan. Reduce heat; simmer 20 minutes, stirring often. Cool. Place half the mixture into a blender container. Add strawberries; blend on high until smooth. Stir mixture into remaining soup; add wine and mix thoroughly. Serve well-chilled.

Makes 4 servings.

CHERRY-RHUBARB GELATIN SALAD

Serve on lettuce leaves.

6 cups rhubarb, cut into ½-inch pieces
1½ cups granulated sugar
2 cups water
1 6-ounce package cherry-flavored gelatin

Topping
1 3-ounce package cream cheese, mixed in a bowl
with ¼ cup mayonnaise and 1 teaspoon granulated sugar

Cook rhubarb, sugar and water in a saucepan, stirring often, until rhubarb is tender. Stir in dry gelatin into hot mixture. Pour into a mold or a 13x9-inch glass baking dish. Refrigerate until set. Serve with cream cheese topping. Refrigerate leftovers.

Makes 8 servings.

MARY DOW'S RHUBARB SALAD

Serve with additional thawed whipped topping as desired.

4 cups fresh rhubarb, chopped
1½ cups granulated sugar
½ cup water
1 6-ounce package strawberry-flavored gelatin (dry)
1 8-ounce crushed pineapple, well-drained
2 cups frozen strawberries
1 8-ounce container frozen non-dairy whipped topping
1 cup miniature marshmallows
½ teaspoon pure vanilla extract

Cook rhubarb, sugar and water in a saucepan, stirring often, until rhubarb is tender. Stir in dry gelatin, pineapple, strawberries, whipped topping, marshmallows and vanilla until blended. Pour into a 13x9-inch glass baking dish or bowl. Chill until set. Refrigerate leftovers.

Makes 8 servings.

ORANGE AND RHUBARB SALAD

Top with sweetened whipped cream when serving.

4 cups fresh rhubarb, chopped
½ cup water
1 3-ounce package orange-flavored gelatin (dry)
1 cup granulated sugar
1 3-ounce package cream cheese, cut up
1 11-ounce can Mandarin oranges, drained
1 cup miniature marshmallows

Bring rhubarb and water to a boil in a saucepan. Reduce heat, simmer, stirring often until rhubarb is soft, about 8 minutes. Remove from heat. Stir in dry gelatin until dissolved. Stir in sugar and cream cheese until blended. Stir in oranges and marshmallows. Pour mixture into a 2-quart glass bowl. Chill until set. Refrigerate leftovers.

Makes 6 servings.

ORANGE-RHUBARB SALAD

Serve with a dab of whipped salad dressing, if desired.

2 cups fresh rhubarb, sliced
½ cup water
½ cup granulated sugar
1 3-ounce package orange-flavored gelatin
1 3-ounce package cream cheese, softened
⅔ cup celery, finely diced
⅓ cup pecans, chopped

Bring rhubarb, water and sugar to a boil in a saucepan. Reduce heat; simmer 10 minutes, stirring often. In a bowl, mix dry gelatin and cream cheese until smooth; stir into hot rhubarb until dissolved. Pour into a glass bowl. Chill until thickened slightly, but not set. Stir in celery and pecans. Chill until firm. Refrigerate leftovers.

Makes about 4 half pints.

RASPBERRY-RHUBARB GELATIN SALAD

Serve on lettuce leaves, and top with a dab of salad dressing.

1 cup fresh rhubarb, chopped
¾ cup water
⅓ cup granulated sugar
1 3-ounce package raspberry-flavored gelatin
1 tablespoon raspberry jam
1 cup unsweetened pineapple juice
1 medium-sized tart apple, peeled and diced
½ cup walnuts, chopped

Bring rhubarb, water and sugar to a boil in a saucepan over medium-high heat. Reduce heat, cover and simmer until rhubarb is tender, about 8 minutes. Remove from heat. Stir in dry gelatin until dissolved. Stir in jam. Stir in pineapple juice. Chill until slightly thickened, but not set. Stir in diced apple and walnuts. Pour into six ½-cup molds or a 1-quart mold, coated with nonstick cooking spray. Chill until set. Refrigerate leftovers.

Makes 6 servings.

RHUBARB SPINACH SALAD

A sweet and sour salad.

4 stalks fresh rhubarb, cut diagonally into thin slices
¼ cup granulated sugar

2 tablespoons red-wine vinegar
salt and ground black pepper to taste
6 tablespoons olive oil
4 cups fresh spinach leaves

Place rhubarb in a wide saucepan. Sprinkle with sugar. Cover with water by 1 inch. Bring to a boil over high heat. Boil uncovered for exactly 2 minutes. Remove from heat. Drain rhubarb and reserve liquid.

Place liquid in same saucepan. Stir in vinegar, salt and black pepper. Cook uncovered over high heat until mixture is reduced to ½ cup. Remove from heat; whisk in olive oil.

Place spinach on 4 salad plates; top each with rhubarb. Pour warm salad dressing over salad. Serve immediately.

Makes 4 servings.

ROASTED RHUBARB SALAD

This unusual salad recipe comes from La Porte, Texas.

1 pound fresh rhubarb, cut into 3-inch pieces
1 small shallot, minced
3 tablespoons honey
1 tablespoon red wine vinegar
½ teaspoon salt
½ teaspoon freshly ground black pepper

3 tablespoons extra-virgin olive oil
6 cups mixed salad greens
Manchego cheese or any other firm cheese

Preheat oven to 400°.
Mix rhubarb, shallot, honey, vinegar, salt and black pepper in an ungreased, shallow baking dish. Bake 10 to 12 minutes or until rhubarb is soft but not falling apart. Remove from oven; spoon on a plate and let cool. Pour cooled juice from baking dish into a small bowl. Whisk in olive oil.

Place salad greens on 4 salad plates. Top each with rhubarb; drizzle each with dressing. Top with cheese as desired.

Makes 4 servings.

STRAWBERRY-RHUBARB GELATIN SALAD

Top with whipped cream when serving.

4 cups fresh rhubarb, diced
1½ cups water
½ cup granulated sugar
1 6-ounce package strawberry-flavored gelatin
1 cup fresh orange juice
1 teaspoon freshly grated orange rind
1 cup fresh strawberries, sliced

Cook rhubarb, water and sugar in a saucepan, stirring often, until rhubarb is tender, about 5 minutes. Remove from heat; stir in dry gelatin until dissolved. Stir in orange juice and rind. Chill until thick, but not set. Stir in strawberries. Pour into lightly oiled 6-cup mold or in a bowl. Chill until set. Refrigerate leftovers.

Makes 8 servings.

Beverages

RHUBARB ICED TEA

For flavor variation, add a cinnamon stick when cooking, and stir in fresh lemon juice when serving.

8 stalks rhubarb, cut into 3-inch pieces
8 cups water
⅓ cup granulated sugar, or to taste

Bring rhubarb and water to a boil in a large saucepan. Reduce heat; simmer 1 hour. Strain; discard pulp. Stir sugar into the hot liquid until dissolved. Cool. Serve over ice. Garnish with mint or lavender sprigs.

Makes 6 servings.

RHUBARB PUNCH

The base can be frozen, and ginger ale added when ready to be used.

4 cups fresh rhubarb
½ cup granulated sugar
2 cups water
1 6-ounce container frozen lemonade
3 cups ginger ale or citrus soda, chilled

Cook rhubarb, sugar and water until rhubarb is mushy. Strain; discard pulp. Add frozen lemonade to hot liquid; stir. Add ginger ale when ready to serve. Serve over ice. Refrigerate.

Makes 6 servings.

RHUBARB SLUSH PUNCH

Use other gelatin flavor if desired.

8 cups rhubarb, chopped
8 cups water
2 cups granulated sugar
1 3-ounce package strawberry-flavored gelatin (dry)
½ teaspoon fresh lemon juice

Cook rhubarb and water in a large nonreactive saucepan over medium heat, stirring occasionally, until very soft, about 20 minutes. Strain and discard pulp; return liquid to saucepan. Heat liquid, then add remaining ingredients; stir until sugar and gelatin dissolve.

Freeze mixture in a 2-quart plastic food container. When serving, put frozen punch in a punch bowl, and add 2 quarts ginger ale. Serve.

Makes about 1½ quarts.

RHUBARB WINE

As in all recipes for rhubarb, use only the stalks; discard leaves and roots...they are poisonous.

8 pounds fresh rhubarb, cut into small pieces
8 quarts boiling water
6 pounds granulated sugar
2 12-ounce packages seedless raisins
4 fresh lemons, sliced
4 fresh oranges, sliced
2 yeast cakes

Place rhubarb in a large sterilized crock. Pour boiling water over rhubarb. Cover and let stand one week, stirring well each day. At the end of the week, strain, and add sugar, raisins, lemons, oranges and crumbled yeast cakes to the liquid. Let stand until it stops working, approximately four weeks. (Could be less time if weather is warm.) Strain through several thickness of cheesecloth. Bottle and keep in a cool place.

Makes about 6 quarts.

STRAWBERRY-RHUBARB LEMONADE

Serve this refreshing lemonade over ice in tall glasses.

3½ cups water
2 cups fresh rhubarb, cut into 1-inch pieces
¾ cup granulated sugar, or to taste
2 3-inch strips fresh lemon zest
½ teaspoon pure vanilla extract
2 cups strawberries, sliced and divided
1 cup fresh lemon juice

Bring water, rhubarb, sugar, lemon zest and vanilla to a boil in a nonreactive saucepan, stirring until sugar is dissolved. Reduce heat; cover and simmer 8 minutes. Stir in 1 cup strawberries. Bring to a boil; cover and boil 2 minutes. Cool, then strain through a coarse sieve over a serving pitcher; discard pulp. Stir in remaining strawberries and lemon juice. Refrigerate.

Makes 6 servings.

Sauces
Condiments

BLUEBERRY-RHUBARB BREAKFAST SAUCE

Great breakfast treat...serve with waffles, toast, pancakes, etc.

6 cups finely fresh rhubarb, chopped
4 cups granulated sugar
1 21-ounce can blueberry pie filling
1 3-ounce package raspberry-flavored gelatin

Bring rhubarb and sugar to a boil in a nonreactive saucepan. Boil 10 minutes, stirring often. Stir in pie filling; bring to a boil. Remove from heat; stir in dry gelatin. Spoon into sterilized jars. Refrigerate up to 1 week or freeze in plastic food containers.

Makes about 7 cups.

MICROWAVE RHUBARB SAUCE

That's an easy treat.

2 cups fresh rhubarb, diced
2 cups granulated sugar

Stir rhubarb and sugar in a large microwave-safe bowl. Cook on high 12 minutes, stirring every 3 minutes. Serve warm over ice cream. Or refrigerate for later use, no longer than 1 week.

Makes about 1 cup.

ORANGE-RHUBARB SAUCE

Serve over ice cream, pudding or pound cake.

2 pounds fresh rhubarb, cut into 1-inch pieces
¾ cup granulated sugar
⅓ cup fresh orange juice
1 teaspoon freshly grated orange rind
¼ teaspoon ground nutmeg
¼ teaspoon salt
½ teaspoon pure vanilla extract

Bring all ingredients except vanilla to a boil in a large saucepan. Reduce heat to low. Cover and simmer, stirring often, about 15 minutes. Stir in vanilla. Cool to room temperature. Serve or refrigerate no longer than 2 weeks before using.

Makes about 3½ cups.

PINEAPPLE-RHUBARB SAUCE

Delicious over pound cake and other desserts.

3 cups fresh rhubarb, cut into ½-inch pieces
1 8-ounce can crushed pineapple, drained, juice reserved
¼ cup granulated sugar, or to taste
½ teaspoon ground ginger
½ teaspoon pure vanilla extract
1 tablespoon cornstarch, dissolved in 2 tablespoons water

Cook rhubarb and reserved juice, covered, in a saucepan over low heat, stirring often, until tender; add pineapple. Stir in sugar, ginger and vanilla. Add cornstarch mixture, stirring constantly; boil 1 minute. Serve or spoon into a glass jar; refrigerate covered.

Makes about 1½ cups.

RASPBERRY-RHUBARB SAUCE

Serve at room temperature.

½ cup granulated sugar
½ cup water
2 cups fresh rhubarb, cut into ¼-inch slices
½ teaspoon pure vanilla extract
1 cup fresh raspberries, quartered

Simmer sugar and water in a saucepan until sugar is dissolved. Add rhubarb; simmer, stirring often, 5 minutes or until rhubarb is tender; stir in vanilla. Place mixture into a glass bowl. Stir in raspberries. Serve or refrigerate no more than 1 week before using.

Makes about 1½ cups.

RED CURRANT-RHUBARB SAUCE

The sauce for wild game.

2 cups fresh rhubarb, peeled and diced into ¼-inch pieces
1¼ cups red currant jelly
1 tablespoon arrowroot
1 tablespoon port wine

Cook rhubarb and currant jelly in a saucepan, stirring often, over medium heat until reduced by about a third. Strain the rhubarb out of the sauce. Discard pulp. There should be 1 cup of liquid. If there is more than 1 cup, continue to reduce liquid over medium heat to 1 cup total. Mix arrowroot and wine, stirring out any lumps. Bring the sauce to a boil. Add wine mixture; stir constantly for 1 minute. Reduce heat; simmer 2 minutes. Serve or spoon in a clean jar; cover and refrigerate.

Makes about 1 cup.

RHUBARB SAUCE

A versatile sauce…good over ice cream or chicken.

1¼ cups granulated sugar
1 tablespoon water
1 tablespoon finely shredded orange peel
6 cups fresh rhubarb slices ¼-inch thick
½ teaspoon pure vanilla extract

Mix sugar, water and orange peel in a saucepan. Bring to a boil. Add rhubarb. Reduce heat and simmer, uncovered, stirring often, until rhubarb is tender and mixture is thickened, about 8 minutes. Stir in vanilla. Cool. Spoon into clean jars; cover and refrigerate for no more than 1 week, or place in plastic containers and freeze.

Makes about 3½ cups.

STEWED RHUBARB

Try some on your hot breakfast cereal...good.

6 cups fresh rhubarb, chopped
1 cup granulated sugar
2 tablespoons water

Mix all ingredients in a large saucepan. Cook over medium heat, stirring until sugar is dissolved. Reduce heat to medium-low. Simmer uncovered, stirring often, about 15 minutes or until slightly thickened and rhubarb is in threads. Cool. Refrigerate up to 5 days.

Makes about 3 cups.

STRAWBERRY-RHUBARB DESSERT SAUCE

Delicious on cake, pudding, ice cream and other desserts.

3 cups fresh rhubarb, cut into 1-inch pieces
1 cup granulated sugar
⅓ cup water
1 cup fresh strawberries, halved

1 tablespoon cornstarch, dissolved in 2 tablespoons water
1 teaspoon pure vanilla extract

Bring rhubarb, sugar and water to a boil in a saucepan. Reduce heat; cover and simmer 5 minutes, stirring often. Add strawberries; cook until tender, about 3 minutes. Add dissolved cornstarch to rhubarb mixture. Cook, stirring constantly, until mixture boils and thickens. Remove from heat; stir in vanilla. Spoon into clean glass jar; cover. Chill. Refrigerate leftovers.

Makes about 3 cups.

STRAWBERRY-RHUBARB TOPPING

Serve this good topping, warm or chilled, over custard, ice cream, pound cake and other desserts.

4 cups fresh rhubarb, cut into 1-inch pieces
½ cup granulated sugar
⅓ cup water
2½ teaspoons cornstarch dissolved in 1 tablespoon water in a cup
3 cups fresh strawberries, sliced
1 teaspoon pure vanilla extract

In a saucepan, over medium heat, bring rhubarb, sugar and water to a boil. Reduce heat; simmer, uncovered, until rhubarb is tender, about 6 minutes. Add cornstarch mixture, stirring constantly until mixture boils. Cook and stir until thickened. Remove from heat; stir in strawberries and vanilla extract. Refrigerate.

Makes 5 servings.

JALAPENO RHUBARB CHUTNEY

For more heat, add more jalapeno.

1 pound rhubarb, cut into ¼-inch thick slices
2 teaspoons coarsely grated fresh ginger
2 cloves garlic
1 jalapeno chile, seeds and membranes removed, chopped
1 tablespoon ground paprika
1 tablespoon black mustard seeds
¼ cup currants
1 cup light brown sugar, packed
1½ cups white vinegar

Place all the ingredients in a nonreactive pan. Bring to a boil; reduce heat and simmer until rhubarb is tender and texture of jam, about 30 minutes. Spoon mixture into a clean glass jar; cover. Refrigerate.

Makes about 1 cup.

RHUBARB ONION CHUTNEY

Tangy and sweet.

1½ pounds onions, halved lengthwise and cut crosswise
    into ¼-inch slices
3 tablespoons corn oil

1 cup golden raisins
½ cup hot water
3 tablespoons red wine vinegar
⅛ teaspoon ground cloves
½ cup granulated sugar
3 cups fresh rhubarb, cut into ½-inch pieces
salt and ground black pepper to taste

Place onions and oil in a large saucepan over medium-low heat. Cook, stirring occasionally, until softened.

Mix raisins, hot water, vinegar, cloves and sugar in a bowl; let stand 15 minutes; stir mixture into the onions. Bring to a boil, stirring constantly; sprinkle with rhubarb; cook at a slow boil 5 minutes. Stir and cook uncovered about 5 minutes or until rhubarb is tender. Season with salt and black pepper to taste. Spoon into clean jars; cover and refrigerate for no more than 1 week. Serve warm or at room temperature.

Makes about 3 cups.

RHUBARB-PLUM CHUTNEY

This chutney is delicious served with grilled pork or chicken.

1 tablespoon mustard seeds
1 pound rhubarb, cut into ½-inch pieces
3 medium plums, cut into ½-inch pieces
¼ cup golden raisins
¼ cup granulated sugar
⅓ cup cider vinegar
1 tablespoon fresh ginger, chopped

Toast mustard seeds in a nonreactive saucepan over low heat until they pop. Remove pan from heat. Add remaining ingredients. Bring to a simmer, and cook until rhubarb and plums are tender, about 8 minutes. Remove from heat; let cool. Spoon chutney into a clean jar; cover and store in refrigerator for no longer than 2 weeks.

Makes about 2 cups.

WALNUT RHUBARB CHUTNEY

Serve this tangy chutney with cheese and French bread or crackers.

2 cups golden brown sugar, packed
¾ cup cider vinegar
¼ cup water
1 tablespoon chopped lemon zest

6 rhubarb stalks, trimmed, cut into 1-inch slices
1 4-inch cinnamon stick, broken into smaller pieces
1 1-inch piece fresh ginger, peeled and minced
1 cup golden raisins
⅔ cup walnuts, coarsely chopped
¼ teaspoon salt

Stir first four ingredients in a heavy stainless steel saucepan over low heat until sugar is dissolved. Add rhubarb, cinnamon and ginger. Cook over medium heat, stirring often, until rhubarb is tender, about 10 minutes. Stir in raisins, walnuts and salt. Stir and cook 3 minutes. Spoon chutney into clean jars; cover and refrigerate for no more than 2 weeks, or place in plastic containers and freeze.

Makes about 4 cups.

RHUBARB KETCHUP

Try this ketchup on your next batch of French fries.

4 cups fresh rhubarb, diced
3 medium onions, chopped
1 cup white vinegar
1 cup brown sugar, packed
1 cup granulated sugar
1 28-ounce can tomatoes with liquid, cut up
2 teaspoons salt
1 teaspoon ground cinnamon
1 teaspoon pickling spice

Cook all ingredients in a large nonreactive saucepan, stirring occasionally until thick, about 1 hour. Spoon into a sterilized glass jar; cover and store in refrigerator up to 1 week.

Makes about 2 cups.

RHUBARB PICKLES

Pickled rhubarb...it rocks!

2 cups apple cider vinegar
1 tablespoon coarse salt
1½ cups granulated sugar
1 teaspoon whole cloves
1 2-inch piece fresh ginger, peeled and sliced
4 small dried chile peppers (your choice)
1 pound fresh rhubarb, trimmed and cut into 5-inch-long pieces

Mix vinegar, salt and sugar in a stainless steel saucepan. Cook over medium heat, stirring until salt and sugar are dissolved. Add cloves, ginger and chile peppers. Bring mixture to a boil over medium-high heat; boil 1 minute. Pack the rhubarb into a tall glass sterilized jar. Pour the hot mixture over rhubarb to cover completely. Let cool, then cover and refrigerate overnight before using. Refrigerate up to 1 week only.

Makes about 1 pint.

RHUBARB RELISH

Rhubarb relish...good condiment for most meats.

2 cups fresh rhubarb, finely chopped
2 cups onion, finely chopped
2½ cups brown sugar, packed
1 cup white vinegar
1 teaspoon salt
½ teaspoon ground cinnamon
½ teaspoon allspice
¼ teaspoon ground cloves
¼ teaspoon ground black pepper

Mix all ingredients in a nonreactive saucepan. Cook over medium heat, stirring occasionally, about 30 minutes or until thickened. Cool. Spoon into sterilized jar. Cover and store in refrigerator up to 1 week.

Makes about 1 cup.

RHUBARB SALSA

Good with chicken and fish.

2 cups fresh rhubarb, finely diced
½ cup sweet red pepper, chopped
½ cup sweet yellow pepper, chopped
½ cup fresh cilantro
3 green onions, finely chopped
1 chili pepper, minced and seeded
2 tablespoons fresh lime juice
brown sugar to taste
salt to taste
ground black pepper to taste

Blanch rhubarb in a saucepan in boiling water 10 seconds. Strain under cold water; drain. Place in a glass bowl. Add remaining ingredients; mix well. Store in refrigerator no longer than 1 week.

Makes about 2 cups.

Jams
Jelly
Marmalade
Conserves
Preserves

APRICOT-RHUBARB FREEZER JAM

For variety, use strawberry pie filling and strawberry gelatin or cherry pie filling and cherry gelatin.

5 cups fresh rhubarb, cut into ½-inch pieces
1 cup water
5 cups granulated sugar
1 cup canned apricot pie filling
2 3-ounce packages apricot-flavored gelatin dessert mix

Place rhubarb and water in a 6-quart pot; simmer until rhubarb is tender, about 5 minutes; stir in sugar. Bring to a boil; boil 7 minutes. Reduce heat to medium. Stir in pie filling until blended. Stir in gelatin until dissolved. Cool hot mixture, then spoon into freezer containers. Freeze up to 1 year.

Makes about 7 half pints.

BLUEBERRY-RHUBARB JAM

Biscuits topped with blueberry-rhubarb jam...a great way to start the day.

5 cups fresh rhubarb, cut into 1-inch pieces
5 cups granulated sugar
½ cup water
1 21-ounce can blueberry pie filling
2 3-ounce packages raspberry-flavored gelatin dessert mix

Mix rhubarb, sugar and water in a large nonreactive pot; bring to a boil. Boil uncovered, stirring constantly, 3 minutes. Stir in pie filling; return to a boil; boil 6 minutes, stirring constantly. Stir in dry gelatin; boil 3 minutes, stirring constantly.

Pour jam into sterilized jars; seal. Store in refrigerator 2 weeks or in the freezer for up to 1 year.

Makes 8 half pints.

EASY STRAWBERRY-RHUBARB JAM

An easy jam to prepare. Substitute frozen strawberries if desired.
Recipe courtesy of Ms. Hoganson.

4 cups fresh rhubarb, diced
4 cups granulated sugar
1 cup fresh strawberries, cut into small pieces
1 3-ounce package strawberry-flavored gelatin dessert mix

Mix rhubarb, sugar and strawberries in a large saucepan. Bring to a boil, then reduce heat to medium. Cook stirring often, 15 minutes. Remove from heat; stir in dry gelatin. Pour jam into sterilized jars or freezer containers. Store in refrigerator 2 weeks or freeze.

Makes about 3 half pints.

FIGS AND RHUBARB JAM

This would be a good one to make for giving as gifts.

6 quarts fresh rhubarb, cut into 1-inch pieces
1 pound dried figs, cut into fine shreds
11 cups granulated sugar
1 cup mixed candied fruit peel, chopped

Mix rhubarb, figs and sugar in a large glass jar or crock. Cover and let stand 8 hours. Place mixture in a large kettle; boil, stirring often, for 1 hour or until mixture is very thick. Stir in the candied fruit peel just before removing from heat. Remove from heat; pour jam into warm sterilized jars; seal and process for canning.

Makes about 5 half pints.

MICROWAVE STRAWBERRY-RHUBARB JAM

Great for that breakfast toast.

4 cups fresh rhubarb, cut into ½-inch slices
1 quart fresh strawberries
¾ cup granulated sugar

Place rhubarb and strawberries in a large microwave-safe bowl. Sprinkle with sugar and toss until coated. Microwave on high 10–12 minutes. Spoon into sterilized jars. Refrigerate 1 week or freeze.

Makes about 5 cups.

ORIENTAL RHUBARB JAM

Spread this jam on warm orange muffins.

1 pound fresh rhubarb, finely chopped
3 cups granulated sugar
½ teaspoon five-spice powder
¼ cup candied ginger, chopped
⅛ teaspoon hot pepper sauce, scant
3 tablespoons fresh lemon juice

Place all ingredients in a large saucepan; mix well. Cook over low heat, stirring constantly, until sugar dissolves. Bring to a boil; skim off foam, and cook over medium heat, stirring often, until mixture is thickened and clear, about 15–20 minutes. Pour jam into hot sterilized jars; seal. Refrigerate 1 week or freeze.

Makes about 3 half pints.

PEACH-RHUBARB JAM

Frozen unsweetened sliced rhubarb may be use in place of fresh.

2 quarts fresh rhubarb, cut into 1-inch pieces
4 cups granulated sugar
1 21-ounce can peach pie filling
1 6-ounce package orange-flavored gelatin dessert mix

Mix rhubarb and sugar in a large glass bowl; let stand 8 hours. Place mixture into a large saucepan; bring to a boil, then reduce heat and simmer, stirring often, 10 minutes. Dice the canned peaches, and add to saucepan along with the filling; bring to a boil. Remove from heat; stir in dry gelatin until dissolved. Spoon jam into sterilized jars or freezer containers. Cool completely. Refrigerate up to 1 week or freeze.

Makes about 6 half pints.

PINEAPPLE AND RHUBARB JAM

Easy to prepare.

5 cups fresh rhubarb, chopped
4 cups granulated sugar
1 20-ounce can crushed pineapple, drained
1 6-ounce package strawberry-flavored gelatin dessert mix

Mix rhubarb, sugar and pineapple in a large saucepan. Bring to a boil over medium-high heat. Boil, stirring often, 10 minutes. Remove from heat; stir in dry gelatin. Pour jam into warm sterilized jars; seal and process for canning. You can also simply store jam in refrigerator up to 1 week, or pour jam into freezer containers and freeze.

Makes about 6 half pints.

RHUBARB GINGER JAM

Crystallized ginger gives this rhubarb jam a special flavor.

1 16-ounce package frozen sliced rhubarb (do not thaw)
1¼ cups granulated sugar
3 tablespoons chopped crystallized ginger
1 teaspoon freshly grated lemon peel

Mix all ingredients in a heavy saucepan. Stir over medium-high heat until sugar dissolves. Bring to a boil, then reduce heat to medium. Simmer, stirring often, until mixture thickens and mounds on a spoon, about 20 minutes. Pour jam in warm sterilized jar; cover and chill. Refrigerate up to 1 week or freeze.

Makes 1½ cups.

RHUBARB-RASPBERRY JAM

Ground cinnamon can be used in place of ground cardamom, if desired.

4 cups fresh rhubarb, cut into 1-inch pieces
2 cups granulated sugar
1 tablespoon fresh lemon juice
1½ pints fresh raspberries
¼ teaspoon ground cardamom

Mix rhubarb, sugar and lemon juice in a large glass bowl. Cover and refrigerate 8 hours.

Place mixture in a large saucepan. Simmer, stirring often, until sugar is dissolved. Bring to a boil and stir often, until mixture thickens slightly, about 5 minutes. Add raspberries; boil, stirring often, until thick, about 6 minutes. Remove from heat; stir in cardamom. Cool completely. Store covered in the refrigerator up to 1 week or freeze.

Makes about 2 cups.

STRAWBERRY-RHUBARB FREEZER JAM

Strawberry-rhubarb jam over waffles…breakfast call.

1 pint fully ripe strawberries
1 cup fresh rhubarb, ground
4 cups granulated sugar

¾ cup water
1 box fruit pectin

Crush strawberries, one layer at a time in a large bowl. Add ground rhubarb and sugar; mix well and let stand a few minutes.

Mix water and pectin in a small saucepan; bring to a rolling boil over high heat, stirring constantly; continue to boil 1 minute. Add to fruit mixture; stir until completely dissolved, about 3 minutes. Fill sterilized containers within ½-inch of tops. Wipe off tops. Cool, then freeze up to 1 year. Thaw and keep in refrigerator when using.

Makes about 5 cups.

RHUBARB-STRAWBERRY JELLY

Rhubarb-strawberry jelly...a springtime favorite.

1½ quarts ripe strawberries, cleaned
1½ pounds fresh red rhubarb, cut
   into 1-inch pieces, then ground
½ teaspoon butter, optional
6 cups granulated sugar
6 ounces liquid pectin

Crush strawberries in a saucepan one layer at a time. Place both crushed strawberries and ground rhubarb in a jelly bag; gently squeeze out juice. Measure 3½ cups of juice; place into a large saucepan. Add butter and sugar; mix well. Bring mixture to a boil over high heat, stirring constantly. Immediately stir in pectin. Bring to a full rolling boil, and boil hard 1 minute, stirring constantly. Remove from heat. Quickly skim off foam, and immediately fill sterilized jars, leaving a ¼-inch headspace. Adjust lids and process for canning in a boiling-water canner.

Makes about 7 half pints.

RHUBARB MARMALADE

Lovely on warm, buttered toast.

2 pounds fresh tender rhubarb, cut into 1-inch pieces
grated rinds of 2 lemons
rind of 1 orange, cut into thin strips
4 cups granulated sugar
juice of 2 lemons

Mix rhubarb, lemon rind, orange rind and sugar in a large glass bowl; let stand 8 hours. Pour mixture into a large saucepan. Add lemon juice. Cook over medium heat, stirring often, until thickened. Immediately pour into hot sterilized jelly glasses. Cover with a thin layer of melted paraffin. When hardened, seal with a cover. Store in refrigerator or freeze.

Makes about 4 half pints.

RHUBARB CONSERVE

Choose any nuts for this rhubarb conserve.

2 pounds fresh rhubarb, cut into 1-inch pieces
2 oranges, rinds grated and juice extracted
1 lemon, rind grated and juice extracted
3½ cups granulated sugar
½ cup chopped nuts

Place all ingredients except nuts in a saucepan over low heat; cook, stirring often, until sugar is dissolved. Continue simmering, stirring constantly, until mixture is thick and clear. Stir in nuts; cook and stir 5 minutes. Pour into sterilized jars; process for canning or freeze.

Makes about 4 cups.

RHUBARB-STRAWBERRY CONSERVE

The bold flavor of rhubarb with sweet strawberries in this conserve.

2 cups granulated sugar
½ cup water
4 cups fresh rhubarb, cut into 1-inch pieces
1 pint fresh strawberries, halved
½ cup walnuts, coarsely chopped
¼ cup golden raisins

Bring sugar and water to a boil in a 3-quart saucepan, stirring constantly. Add rhubarb; boil gently, stirring often, until thick. Stir in strawberries, walnuts and raisins. Bring to a boil; boil gently 5 minutes. Quickly skim off foam. Immediately pour mixture into hot sterilized jars, leaving ¼-inch head-space. Wipe rims; seal. Process for canning; or store in refrigerator up to 1 week, or pour into freezer containers and freeze.

Makes about 4 half pints.

RHUBARB AND FIG PRESERVES

Hot buttermilk biscuits and rhubarb-fig preserves...a breakfast treat!

3½ quarts fresh rhubarb, cut into 1-inch pieces
8 cups granulated sugar
1 pint chopped figs
1 lemon, juice and rind, cut into strips

Mix rhubarb and sugar in a large glass bowl; let stand 8 hours. In a saucepan, combine rhubarb-sugar mixture, figs, lemon juice and rind. Bring to a rapid boil; cook, stirring constantly, until mixture is thick and clear. Immediately pack into hot sterilized jars. Seal immediately and process for canning.

Makes about 4 half pints.

RHUBARB-PINEAPPLE PRESERVES

The rhubarb-pineapple combination for this recipe was suggested
my neighbor, Jeanne. Good on toast, and also on ice cream!

5 cups fresh rhubarb, finely chopped
3½ cups granulated sugar
1 8-ounce can crushed pineapple
2 cups strawberries, sliced
1 6-ounce package strawberry-flavored gelatin

Bring rhubarb, sugar and pineapple to a boil in a heavy saucepan. Reduce
heat. Add strawberries; simmer, stirring occasionally, 25 minutes. Stir in dry
gelatin until dissolved. Pour into sterilized jars. Refrigerate up to 1 week or
freeze in plastic food containers.

Makes about 5 cups.

RHUBARB PRESERVES

Rhubarb preserves, a nice spread for toast.

3 cups granulated sugar
½ cup cold water
4 cups fresh rhubarb, cut into small pieces

Boil sugar and water in a saucepan for 4–5 minutes. Add rhubarb; let simmer about 3 minutes. Pour syrup and rhubarb mixture into a sterilized jar. Refrigerate, freeze or process for canning.

Makes about 1 pint.

About the Author

Theresa Millang is a popular and versatile cookbook author. She has written successful cookbooks on muffins, brownies, pies, cookies, cheesecake, casseroles, and several on Cajun cooking. She has cooked on television, and contributed many recipes to food articles throughout the U.S.A.

Theresa's Other Cookbooks
I Love Cheesecake
I Love Pies You Don't Bake
The Muffins Are Coming

Theresa's Other Current Cookbooks
The Best of Cajun-Creole Recipes
The Best of Chili Recipes
The Great Minnesota Hot Dish
The Joy of Blueberries

Notes